KT-590-206

LETTERS FROM SYRIA

BOOK
PRODUCTION
WAR ECONOMY
STANDARD

THIS BOOK IS PRODUCED
IN COMPLETE CONFORMITY WITH
THE AUTHORIZED ECONOMY STANDARDS

By the Same Author

BAGHDAD SKETCHES
THE VALLEYS OF THE ASSASSINS
THE SOUTHERN GATES OF ARABIA
SEEN IN THE HADHRAMAUT
A WINTER IN ARABIA

Freya Stark

FREYA STARK

LETTERS
FROM SYRIA

JOHN MURRAY
ALBEMARLE STREET, LONDON, W.

First Edition . . . 1942

Printed in Great Britain by
Wyman & Sons, Ltd., London, Fakenham and Reading.

CONTENTS

*The two friends go by car to Baalbek and Damascus.
Their next expedition is an unconventional and adventurous
one, seeing that the Druse revolt of August, 1925, had
continued until March, 1927, and that the French rulers of
Syria were far from welcoming intruders. They are mounted
on donkeys and with a Druse guide called Najm make a
leisurely progress towards Palestine. At the end of eleven
days they are at Bosra. There they dismiss their guide and
take a car for Jericho and Jerusalem.*

*These letters re-introduce some persons and places already
familiar to the reader, who will perhaps discern in the last
sentence of all a link with the opening chapter of 'Baghdad
Sketches.'*

LIST OF ILLUSTRATIONS

(From photographs by Miss Venetia Buddicom, except Frontispiece and those otherwise marked)

———

Freya Stark   Frontispiece

———

vii

FOREWORD

THESE letters, written on my first coming to Asia, were neatly and dreamlessly at rest in Sir John Murray's cupboard when, between one blitz and another, the Publisher's eye fell upon them. They were asked for and obtained: the dislocation of war between me and the printer made the sending of proofs impracticable: Sir Sydney Cockerell has most kindly edited them and seen them through the Press.

When they appear, they will be scarcely more known to me than to their readers, for fourteen years have gone by since they were written. They describe that "first fine careless rapture," the opening of the East to eyes that had never left Europe.

This East has now become part of the texture of life, familiar and intimate. Like the face of an old love, it has lost the quality of surprise which first enchanted, which is there no doubt, if the spirit were not too sleepy to be aware of it. We take for granted the infinite variety that we expect.

Yet the freshness trembles beneath the surface of Everyday, a joy perpetual to all who catch its opal lights beneath the dust of habit. I now know that the camel train will come padding under loads of straw round some sharp corner of Lebanon or Anti-Lebanon—asphalted and crowded with lorries of our Yeomanry from home—yet the habitual sight has not lost its magic; the years have added to it a tenderness, a blossoming of all the times when my own pilgrim life has hailed the caravan that bobs noiseless here and there against the burnt Asiatic background. So it is, I think, with most things. Familiarity rather than novelty is what touches our hearts—the revelation of a harmony between ourselves and outward things.   Possibly the joy of discovery is not that of discovery at all in the sense of strangeness; but rather the sudden knowledge that we are at home in a new horizon, whether it be outward or inward, enfranchised in a land in which we are expected and which our heart or brain, experienced but forgetful traveller, recognizes with joy.

BAGHDAD.   F. S.

LETTERS *from* SYRIA

Sketch Map

Scale of Miles

HAWES

1.—FROM VENICE TO BEIRUT. LETTERS 1—12

In the first of these letters Freya Stark has left her home at Asolo and has set out from Venice on a small cargo vessel for her first journey east of Italy and her first contact with the Near East. The s.s. Abbazia *takes her as far as Rhodes, where she spends a few days before proceeding on s.s* Diana *to Beirut. The whole passage occupies three weeks. In the course of it she describes her first impressions of many famous places.*

1.   *To her Mother.*

s.s. *Abbazia*, FIUME.   19.11.27.

DEAREST B.,

All well so far and a very comfy night. They have changed my cabin, as I thought the anchor was falling on my head through the deck.

Only five other passengers. Young Irish couple, talk in whispers only to themselves: young Austrian steamship agent going to Egypt; elderly Turinese business man, attitude entirely commercial; and a German-American with an impressive domed head.

I sit between the Chief Engineer and the Captain, who must have some Turk in him; he is a jovial old boy, with black lips and an immense stomach.

This town has nothing worth seeing but its frontier— just a canal right through it, very disagreeable to live near in war time.

Weather rainy, sirocco, and the sea looks horrid, full of small angry waves.

I hope for news at Brindisi.

Ever so much love to both dear people.

FREYA.

B

2.   *To Miss Buddicom in India.*

s.s. *Abbazia*, NEARING BRINDISI.   23.11.27.

DEAREST VENETIA,

You will just be arriving, and here am I—already twenty-four hours belated by weather, and looking forward to a fearful tossing to-night between Brindisi and Corinth. I had no idea of all the incidents boats are subject to.   First a mild steady rain in Fiume made it impossible to load our cargo of sugar for Egypt.   It cleared at Spalato, where we spent a charming day, eating the food of the country and visiting the market, and admiring Diocletian's taste in country houses.   I think he and Herbert Olivier would have understood each other.   What you want in a ruin is that it should give a feeling of magnificence passed away and of the lapse of time—and that is why it is better without too much restoration.   The odd columns and arcades of Diocletian are let in among the fronts and backs of Spalato houses, until you come to the only clear space, where the Mausoleum stands, very simple and grand, with a court of broken pillars round it.   The same at Bari.   Two marvellous old churches; you could not say whether Romanesque or Byzantine, but huge and empty and fallen one feels on sadder days.   The smaller windows still have the carved stone instead of glass, and a marble elephant is leaning happily out of one of the walls to support a Norman arch on his back.   I wish you had been there, if only to see the colour of the whitewashed piazza in the twilight.

We are now running under the lee of the shore and shall be all right till we cross from Brindisi into the open.   After that, I hear a sailor say: "They will dedicate all their dollars to the Madonna."

It was bad enough before Bari; and last night, when the hawser which was to tow us off the quay into the middle of the harbour broke and could not be fastened to the buoy again because of the rough sea (and Bari has no tug), we all felt much relieved.   It was pleasant to hear the wind in the rigging and us safe in port.

Besides our cargo of cement and sugar, our decks are crammed with barrels of oil, matches, figs, almonds, and soap, which are soused every few minutes till I expect the soap to lather through the chinks.

I have a good book: *The Medieval Conquest of Greece*, by Sir R. Rodd. But I scarce want to read. It is so wonderful to be away, really away; a new land opening out every morning. Pleasant to wander in strange places and come back to one's boat all lighted up and warm and feeling very like a home.

I had a thrilling sight as we left Spalato at night. Just before getting into my bunk I put my head through the porthole, expecting solitude and night outside; and lo and behold, there was a boat lashed on below—a red boat with two boys smoking inside it and surrounded by a lather of foam as we carried it along. It was brilliantly lit by a lamp from our deck and shone out in the general blackness; and presently a man climbed down our side and they unwound the thick hawser and drifted away; they gave a call and were away in the night, with I can't tell you what flavour of adventure and mystery. It was just the pilot being dropped.

Here is Brindisi.

My dear love, FREYA.

3. *To her Father in Canada.*

s.s. *Abbazia*, IN SIGHT OF CORFU. 24.11.27.

DEAREST PIPS,

Can you imagine what a moment it was this morning when, expecting nothing but open sea, I stepped out on deck, and there was Corfu with all its mountains, and behind it the ranges of Epirus with a dark-blue sea in front, and gulls with the sun on their backs circling round us. And this is Greece, too. I suppose no other country would give one quite that sense of joy and wonder. It looks wild enough. A few villages here and there where the hills slope more gently, but mostly great ridges, barren of everything except the travelling shadows.

We are going very slowly—nine miles an hour; and there is a little swell which keeps me happiest in my deck chair. The stewardess compliments me on my staunchness in taking a bath every day. The truth is, I should be sad to have to miss one of these delicious meals; I have not eaten so much for years, and so far the luck has been with us for we have been dining in port or just after starting, before the rolling begins.

We kept a crowd of people waiting at Brindisi, which is a poor sort of place with straight streets, though rather pleasant because of the whitewash or coloured houses, which fade agreeably. We had nothing to load there except a Marconi signal for Turkey, now choking up our deck. And lucky we are it isn't pigs, for the Captain was telling us last night how he brought three deckloads of animals out of the Black Sea and how disgusted his passengers were.

Later.

We are now among islands in the Ionian Sea. Is not the very name an enchantment? The sea is quiet, the twilight falling. I asked for the name of an island on the right. "Ithaca," says the Captain, as if the name were mere geography. And there it is, with a hill rising sheer, and a little sandy cove and village above, cypresses and olives, bare and poor; and Penelope no doubt in the square villa with the well-kept garden. Islands on islands there are, melting away into the night. They are all incredibly steep, many with great cliffs, and wild land at the back, bare ranges. One can see the early adventurers, slipping on from one inlet to the next, as we would turn the corners of a road, in this landlocked sea.

UNDER SALAMIS. 25TH NOV.

After Corinth the land sinks down and a long straight cut is made through tufa, like a slice out of a cake, five miles between sloping walls. We got up at three to see it, only to hear that the current was running too fast and we must wait for daybreak; and so we saw sunrise, rather pale, over Corinth. Our American's comment as we crept between those sheer walls was rather nice: "I guess I can give a tip to the Greek government to put advertisements all along this canal."

We are just under a precipitous ridge of Salamis where

I have invented Xerxes' seat, and the inaccurate information has been taken solemnly by all the Germans standing round.

Your FREYA.

4. *To her Father*.

s.s. *Abbazia*. 26.11.27.

DEAREST PIPS,

We lost the Cyclades in the darkness of the night, and these are the Sporades all round us now. And I am thinking of shedding my leather waistcoat in this good, warm sun. There is a bit of a roll, but nothing vicious, merely life and jollity; and the sea is deep blue, like nothing I have ever seen—the sort of blue that black would turn to if it could. The boat is picking up stranger-looking passengers at every port now: florid gentlemen who try to suppress their curls with brilliantine, and go in for lovely patterns in socks and ties.

I am wishing all day long that you were with me. Yesterday on the Acropolis, if only to see the colour of that marble. It used to be painted a deep ochre, and now there is still a tawny shadow in the sheltered places, and the rest just the colour of sunlight. There is a little Ionic temple so delicate, it might be lace-work in stone. But oh, the beautiful Doric!

Greek history came back to me in bits as the old names were repeated; Phalerum where the old walls went, and Hymettus and the way to Marathon beyond. There is still the mark of the old footsteps on the way up to sacrifice. The whole place is beautifully left alone: no labels, no railings: if you become absent-minded in admiration, you can easily step backwards from the Acropolis into space. We had only three hours—enough to know that one must see it again. Some day at sunset or sunrise, or if one could climb up with the moon.

I had no idea of what a large town Athens is; over a million inhabitants, and full of contrasts: wide asphalt roads jerking one off into knobbly side streets at a risk of life. Piraeus is a big harbour full of amusement. The

people swarmed up our side as soon as they could, yelling
and quarrelling with all the noisiness, cheatsomeness and
general badness that the modern Greek is sometimes
credited with.   We finally got a decent little man with a
sad decayed gentility about him to save us from the other
robbers.

Your FREYA.

5.   *To her Mother.*

RHODES.   27.11.27.

DARLING B.,
        My landing in Rhodes last night was full of emotions.
First of all, it appeared that a visa was necessary, and they
would not let me think of landing till the letter to the
Governor flattened them out.   Then a swarm of Greek
villains clambered up, yelling for luggage and passengers,
out of a dark sea in which lots of shallow boats were
squabbling violently.   I was the only passenger descending,
but my kind Irish helped me out; the *Abbazia* staff kept all
except one brigand at bay, and my luggage joggled down
the gangway.   We followed, with pushing and shouting
around us, till we got clear into the darkness, sliding under
the lantern of the round fort towards the lights of the town.
        My Irish left me to try and find the post office before
joining me at dinner.   I followed my man in the dark over
rough ground to a solitary little house on a promontory
where the Customs and Sanitá live in isolation.   I stumbled
up to it and found one Neapolitan and a guard of swarthy
men in khaki with astrakhan on their heads.   They meant
to look at all I had.   When my big box was opened and
they had got their fingers well among everything, the light
went out.   "This is the habit of the country," thought I,
and wondered what they were abstracting; no one seemed
in a hurry to light again.   Finally a candle came, and was
again nearly put out by the Italian, who could not get his
cigar to burn well.   I got annoyed, especially as I thought
he was going to put his fingers on my revolver.   After that
things went better, and I left with no further examinations.
        The hotel is sumptuous, but also pleasant, though

hideous from outside. My room has bathroom, and white walls with friezes of swallows and wistaria to match the cretonnes and cushions. I look from it across the sea to the hills of Anatolia, ranges and ranges. I thought the hotel looked empty, but the manager said: "No. There were ten people yesterday."

I have now sent my letter to the Governor with a card, and am told that his A.D.C. is coming at seven this evening. More later.

Your own FREYA.

6. *To her Father.*

RHODES. 29.11.27.

DEAREST PIPS,

You have no idea of anything like this island. I came back quite stunned after my first wandering through its streets; I felt I must get inside my ordinary bedroom to make myself at home again in the everyday world.

Think of an armed town complete in its walls and towers, with battlemented bastions at intervals, and gates that let you in by zigzag ways under the arrow slits and catapult emplacements. Right through the middle runs the Knights' way with all its palaces, of France, England, Italy, Spain, Provence. They are practically intact, or carefully restored, and there is nothing else near to spoil them: so that, looking up the hill from the bottom of the street, you can see it just as it used to be, with a Turkish woman or two in white, and only the Knights themselves wanting in the picture.

The walls are built to a great width round the city, and filled in with earth, so that you can walk along a causeway about thirty feet broad and look over all the roofs and minarets inside. A little narrow way, with parapet and arrow slits, and flanked with towers, runs along the outside, two-thirds way up the face of the outer wall; and then there is the ditch, sixty feet broad at least, and raked by the Knights' stone cannon balls from subterranean vaults below the ramparts, and built up on the landward side with another steep wall. Each "language" had a bit of fortification to defend. The Italian piece, which gets its name from one of the Del Carrettos, is the most heavily defended of all, with a long island of solid earthworks between two ditches beyond the actual walls. There used to be sorties from outlets in the vaults, and fighting in the fosse.

The great siege was in the sixteenth century, when the Knights held firm against terrific odds and finally surrendered on honourable terms to Soliman. The bullet holes still spatter pieces of the wall as thick as rain. When the end was coming, and no hope of help from Christians in Europe, one of the Knights came secretly to terms with the enemy; it was discovered just in time, and they hung his head on the outside of the wall for Soliman to see. They had a clever Italian engineer—Martinengo; he invented the first rudimentary field telephone, collecting the sound in shallow hide receptacles which he used to let down by a long string so as to hear where the enemy were digging mines. In the terms of surrender Soliman asked to have him handed over as he had given him so much trouble; but the Knights said that he had died during the siege and smuggled him away.

Outside the fortifications, and making a belt of solitude round them, are Turkish and Jewish graveyards, long grasses growing among neglected tombs. The little upright slabs of stone or marble have the man's fez or turban carved like a knob on the top of them; narcissus and bunches of grey cactus grow there, and the old city is cut away completely from its new suburbs.

Inside it, Jews and Greeks and Turks live in three separate quarters, with narrow streets like Liguria, only brighter because of the universal use of whitewash and the charming habit of paving their courts and living-rooms with bright round pebbles, black and white and a few red, laid together in patterns and kept brilliantly clean. Most of the houses have just this court and a small kitchen, and then one big living-room where they eat and sleep and entertain their friends. The Knights' houses had two or more stories, but otherwise it is unnatural here and does not belong to the country. The Turkish women go about veiled in black or white; the Jewish wear round velvet caps, the shape of a tambourine and very unbecoming; and they are descended from the exiled Jews of Spain and still speak Spanish among themselves.

The most beautiful building of all is the Hospital of the Knights, which they have arranged with great taste as a museum and it is filled with a rich collection of primitive Greek potteries. The Director took me over, explaining, and the whole life of those early traffickers seemed to rise out of their old red and yellow wares. How old is this Mediterranean Sea! It made the great building itself seem of our own time. You climb up to the hall from a massive courtyard with a marble lion in the middle of it and heavy stone portico round; the stairs are without a parapet, like all the old stairways in Rhodes, and they lead you to a great raftered room where the patients were cared for. In the far wall is a little niche of a chapel with fluted pillars, and there are little rooms where the more important pilgrims could be privately attended to. And one wanders out into a little cloistered garden with mosaics and tombs and bits of marble gods lying among the bignonias and geraniums.

Your FREYA.

7. *To her Mother.*

RHODES. 30.11.27.

DARLING B.,

The Governor received me very charmingly and talked for three-quarters of an hour, chiefly about Rhodes and his work here, but also about Turin and Dronero which he knew well. It seems that his sister married Giolitti's son!

My entrance missed fire a little: when the two flaps of the door were to be thrown open to let me in, one of them stuck, and there were His Excellency and I separated by a crouching menial who could not get the thing to work. We both waited, but it was no good. I was finally asked to deign to accept only half a door, which is I believe "*la Petite Entrée,*" but quite sufficient for my figure.

It must be fun to be practically king of an island manageable in size with a population ready to be thankful for any decent government. His Excellency told me that he enjoyed it. He is planning to make it a centre for all Italians of the Levant, and to found a University, of which he shewed me the plan. He does most things himself here, and his taste is fortunately good. The new Government House is a delightful building, in red and yellow Lindos stone which will soon look as if it had always been standing here; and he shewed me over the reception and dining-rooms, for which he had himself planned the decoration. He says he has very little trouble with his people, and that of all of them the Turks are the pleasantest to deal with, obedient, honest and stupid (the three subject virtues). Rather a nice story about them: he wanted a piece of land, but the Turkish owner would not sell because it had been in his family for four hundred years, ever since the conquest. "But," said he, "the Italian Government has always treated us well. Why does it not take the land? We will make no objection."

After my interview, I was handed over to Signor Benetti, the A.D.C., to be looked after and provided with all I can possibly desire, which is being done in the most complete manner. Every morning I am asked what can be done for my amusement. There is an English Air Force couple here, regular service people, on their honeymoon, and very pleasant in a conventional way. Benetti invited us all to motor half across the island to Lindos, which is its second town. It was a long day—8 a.m. to 6 p.m.—over every description of country and roads. I rather believe that what I enjoyed most was dashing across the island and all its ridges on a road which is not yet made, but only planned out, with all its angles and gradients still in their crudest stages: it had all the delights of a switchback with the most amazing landscape to look at between the gasps. It was an old dream of mine, which I now see was only a premonition; I find myself in a car on the brow of a long hill, and the road has suddenly turned to a mule track and goes bang down at an acute angle, and I can't stop. I never come to any harm, and neither did we. The only difference was that here we had an excellent chauffeur instead of myself at the wheel, and that is why I am alive

to write. Mr. D. turned round to his wife at intervals.
"See that corner coming, my dear?" he said. But Mrs.
D. was very pale, and said nothing in a heroic way.

It was lovely country, and a windy day with shadows.
As Rhodes is small, it seems to have made up its mind to
condense all sorts of landscape in a narrow space. We
ran through dry poor lands, thin olives here and there and
neither shade nor water; down into orange groves, and
fruit trees and long grass; and then into Macchia, among
small pines, and cypress of the kind outspread like cedars,
and climbed up on to a high rocky ridge, the island back-
bone, among cool fir woods, old lichen-covered trees where
the air struck cold. The anemones are in bloom, both
the white and the bloodstained ones of the legend; and
leaves everywhere of asphodel and narcissus. And all is
absolutely lonely. The peasants live shut up in villages,
which you come upon with startling suddenness, glittering
white, low and flat-roofed like clusters of boxes.

We stopped at Malona. A beautiful Greek woman took
us to pick tangerines in her garden where the trees grew
in a wilderness among the young shoots of wheat. I
learned to say "Good morning" and "Thank you". The
people are very friendly as we pass. They stretch out
their arms in a Fascist salute to our Government car, and it
seems to go with the country. This is a good Government
indeed for an ignorant and rudimentary people; the
Governor is devoted to them, and no time is wasted in
discursive legislation.

Signor Benetti is Bolognese and knows all our friends,
and now accepts me as mysterious but no longer deplorable.
I suppose no Italian can imagine me to be genuinely
interested in Arabic; except the man at the museum who
can sympathize with lunatics, being an enthusiast himself.

We stopped again to watch a bridge being built. The
women here do all the heavy labour: they were steering
wheelbarrows of gravel up the steep planks.

We came out again to the coast, running by white and
blue bays of sand. Round a sudden corner, Lindos
appeared, an old Acropolis above the sea. The little
white town is on the neck of the promontory, the red rock
over it, not a tree in sight. It belongs to the archaic days,

but only fragments of walls and columns are left, and what remains is the fortress of the Knights, its wall and great stairway, and the sea far below. As you go up the stair, however, you come on the shape of a galley, carved in the cliff, the work of some very early wanderer. I can't tell you what magic of the earliest ages lies on this place; the Knights have gone, but the spirit that still lives here is long before their day. Down below, across a bay as dark as a sapphire, there is a smaller headland, also of red rock; and there is the little dome of Cleobulos who was one of the Seven Sages, and asked to be buried in that loneliness. It is all mystery; but a limpid mystery: the sun and sea and the clear light of the islands; there seemed to be no sadness in these lost ages.

We turned back into the town, escorted by the Maresciallo of Carabiniers whose men were cooking our lunch. He told me what a hot place it is, up to 120 in summer; there is scarce a tree except an olive or two and the sun beats against the red cliffs behind the town. There is a small post of seven carabiniers, and the wretched bureaucrats in Rome refuse to grant them leave to wear drill uniforms and topees in the hot weather. They seemed on very good terms with the people there. They spend their evenings teaching the children Italian, and as we went through the streets with them the women came out to us with little nosegays and greetings.

We called at one of the Greek houses to see Rhodian pottery in its home. It takes its name from Lindos, and there were about thirty of the beautiful plates hanging on the wall. The designs and colours must surely come originally from Persia? The red is made of crushed coral and very rich. These plates are always kept as a dowry for the girls of the family. They are practically unobtainable now; the modern ones cannot get the colour, or anything near it, and the factory at Kuteiba, which was the best imitation, is now closed also, and its wares increasing in value. This was the richest house in the village, with a façade worked all over with delicate traceries, and they were very proud of their treasures. They had a marvel of the old red and green island embroidery and a good rug spread high up in one corner over the nuptial bed. The rest was all cheap prints and cotton covers. The daughter of the house stood before us holding a tray with quince jelly and teaspoons and glasses of water and little glasses of vermouth and comfits. Benetti told us what to do. It is a rite of hospitality. We took a spoonful of jelly; then a sip of water; then all the vermouth; then a sweet. The girl stood before us, one after the other, which must have been very tiring. I was glad I had learnt to say "thank you".

The carabinier then took us to their small barracks where his men had arranged a divan for us on the terrace in front of the view. Meanwhile they were preparing us a gigantic *pasta asciutta*. They were nice simple southerners, very anxious to please Benetti's guests. I had a dreadful lot of polite talking to do as the guest of the Government and the only one there to be happy in either French or Italian. I had to make speeches; and remembered to ask if the Maresciallo might join us at our meal, which pleased Benetti. I am now sending them a box of sweets as the only return I can think of for their kindness.

> Your own FREYA.

8. *To her Mother.*

AT ANCHOR IN RHODES, S.S. *Diana*. 3.12.27.

DARLING B.,

I am away again, feeling that some months in Rhodes might have gone very happily. I had a pleasant morning wandering among the Turkish graves, and home through the old streets, and met a flock of turkeys being herded through the middle of the town, with a melon seed thrown now and then before them to encourage them in the right way. I plucked up courage and walked into the mosque which was once Santa Maria of the Knights; very restful now and dilapidated. The sun streamed in through little round panes of blue and yellow glass and two sparrows were chattering in the dome. I was stooping to take off my shoes when an old man signed to me that it did not matter so long as I avoided the carpets which were all massed in the middle. And so I sat down on a seat and looked at the walls where the peeling plaster is never renewed, and at the untidy sabots strewn about for the feet of the faithful, and at the absurd grandfather clock, and wondered why it was all so harmonious. That was a well-spent morning.

An old Turkish doctor came to call on the D.s—a kindly old gentleman with a black terrier fondly called Fox and the largest turquoise ring and studs you ever saw. He had a sort of rosary of black coral and spent the time passing the beads through his fingers placidly in the pauses —and they were many, for the D.s have only about five words of French between them; they just go on talking English and expect the world to understand. But they are nice young things, and she especially, trying so hard to keep her young husband in bounds of propriety when he gets carried away by his naval reminiscences. He left the navy, but it has remained with him.

I have been looking out at the hills of Anatolia. Benetti says they would shoot any foreigner at sight who should land there. I doubt it. But the Turks keep it all closed against Italians, who are looking that way with obvious appetite. All that I have known to come over from Smyrna since my arrival is a travelling circus, and you will be interested to hear that the lion died of seasickness on the way.

I came out to the *Diana* from tea with the Governor's lady—such a clever little lady, with quick movements like a mouse and a mouse's long nose and narrow face and bright, kind little eyes. I was the only lady to tea with twenty-five students from Italy and a number of stout official gentlemen; and as I was standing just behind her Excellency my hand got kissed twenty-five times also, on false pretences. She is interested in the island embroidery, and is trying to start it again; but there is a difficulty in finding dyes, and the old stitches are nearly lost; only one old woman in the island knows them, and she refuses to part with the secret! It was like an ode of Hafiz to come up to the house, for it was moonlight already, and one approaches it through a formal garden full of roses with a fountain splashing. The house itself is full of lovely things arranged with great taste. She said we must go and spend a winter in Rhodes, and asked me to call on her in Rome, and the Governor also.

The *Diana* had meanwhile anchored outside the harbour and had to be telephoned not to start without me. I was anxious, for a poor man watched his boat steam out the other day without ever recognizing it till it was too late. She was lying about three kilometers out, all lighted up and looking painfully ready to start as I came down, and you can imagine my feelings when I discovered that my deck chair and camping kit, which had been left locked up in the dogana, were not to be had because the man with the key had disappeared. Messages, telephone, sympathy and general interest, a little bad English with various soldiers and Greeks on the jetty of the lonely little custom house; finally a bicycle lamp slowly making its way round the far side of the harbour; the man appeared with the key in his pocket. It was very unreal rowing out in the night under the fort and the windmills on the pier. Three large vessels at anchor were floating like bunches of stars in what looked like a deeper sky below them. The moon was riding through big white clouds over the ramparts.

We have just started now and I am going to bed.

Your own FREYA.

9. *To her Father*.

s.s. *Diana*. 5.12.27.

DEAREST PIPS,

I don't know whether this will be a long letter, for the boat is ploughing along with great slaps of water banging her side and a tinkle of spray at intervals, just like the sound of splintered ice slipping down the slope when you cut steps in a glacier. I was very languid at breakfast, and had to climb to the open air, and looked at Cyprus with a jaundiced eye, only wishing that the wretched island would stand still. It was a kind land, however, for it got between us and the Greco Levante, whatever that may be, and gave us quite a smooth sea till we turned this last corner. Now there is howling in the rigging, and the engines going heavily, and three objectionable Greeks in the saloon.

We had great luck yesterday and put in to Adalia to deposit a cargo of sugar. The Turks are not anxious for visitors and very few ships go there now. To get there one has to follow the coast. You have no idea of the magnificence of Taurus, rushing in wild peaks straight from the sea to anything between three and ten thousand feet. All desolate. No villages, no cultivation; you slip by for hour after hour and at last long for some sign of life. Finally the ground slopes more gently and runs out in a long low red cliff making an immense bay of level and fertile land with the hills at the back. Streams pour themselves over the edge of the cliff into the sea in a series of cascades, and at the bottom of the bay is Adalia. It has old Venetian walls crumbling down into the water, and a shabby clustering town behind, and a sandy cove where boats are drawn up, all painted a dull lacquer red. The only smart objects in sight were the Turkish officers who, to everyone's surprise, allowed me to go ashore. A huge Turk seized the mail bags or what looked like them, and off we went, rowing to the quay.

I then climbed streets as rough as Acceglio, full of big stones, the houses overhanging as gimcrack as you please, though sometimes the lower floor is of good stone and possibly built by the Venetians; above that it is thin laths of wood nailed criss-cross, and it must be chilly when the wind blows from Taurus. I believe the Turks must have been the inventors of bow windows, there were so many, and prettily painted; until you noticed from some splintering corner that there is nothing but lath and plaster underneath. I came on a most interesting gateway in the battlements; the middle arch is damaged but the two side ones are intact, with roofs carved in squares of marble, very delicately. But in the middle of the town the ramparts dwindle away, and their stones are being stacked to use for building, with bits of column among them.

The whole of Adalia is silent and shabby until you come to the market streets, three or four of them together at the top of the hill, and suddenly you realize that this is the centre of a big country. I walked about among the open shops where there seemed to be every gimcrack produce of Europe and every colour of the East; the best were the bakers'; the bread is shovelled out of a sort of black cave at the back and stacked all hot and smelling good, for sale before us. There were fine country people, more serious than Italians or Greeks, but with good-natured faces, and with marvellous sashes and the apache-like caps which Kemal has substituted for the tarboosh.

Women there were, tramping along veiled, with tight trousers and frills round the ankles. Saddlebags and stirrups. The strange language gave it the effect of a walk in a dream. I saw not one European inscription in the town; the only signpost I could understand was over a photographer's, an angel with wings dropping portraits on surprised gentlemen in bowler hats below. There is a mosque with a good minaret made as it were of a sheaf of six round minarets put together. The whole of it must have been coated with blue and green tiles, for one can still see traces of them at the joins. An old man with whom I managed a few words of Arabic, told me it was Seljuk—fourteenth century, I believe.

The Turks had only given me two hours on land. They are very nervous. The sight of my camera was instantly disapproved of. One of the officers on board told me that when Mussolini made one of his more aggressive speeches one of the Lloyd Triestino boats happened to be anchored here. The Turks took it for granted that the ultimatum was on its way and tried to collar her as she was heaving anchor.

I went down again to the harbour after an hour or so and sat waiting for a boat and watching the wireless being unloaded and hauled up the quay by about forty men; one fat headman sang the verses of a chant to which they all responded in chorus: "*La Ilah illa Allah*" was all I could make out.

My old Turk came and rowed me out together with an amiable young Turk in spats and Homburg hat who told me in bad German that he was Director of Commerce. I said his markets were very fine, and we shook hands like friends, and I paid five piastres less to the boatman in consequence.

Your loving FREYA.

C

10.   *To Miss Buddicom in India.*

s.s. *Diana*, MERSINA. 7.12.27.

DEAREST VENETIA,

This is all enchantment. The names alone would satisfy an average mortal. I have seen Taurus from the sea, and turned the headland of Paphos with waves so blue Venus might have been born that minute. I have been told of the excellence of the hotels on Olympus and would have taken the train to Tarsus this morning only the Turkish authorities would not allow. I have seen flying fish—sea-swallows the Italians call them—and have got money out of the Ottoman bank; and decided that Mersina has nothing but a string of camels to recommend it, and its hills at the back; the plain shelves up here, from sand, to scrub, to snow.

These are all open roadsteads; it takes about half an hour to be rowed to or from the *Diana*; luckily the wind is light and from the north.

You have been rolling along in passenger liners and cannot think what a lot of incident is brought into life by a cargo that has to be lifted or lowered out of or into red and yellow lighters at every anchorage.

I have seen the last of my fellow passengers depart, and am now alone in great state with the captain and chief engineer—and rather looking forward to solitude, for I have never been so much talked to in my life before; the Eastern Mediterranean is simply crowded with friends.

Yesterday in Larnaca I was seized upon by a fat Greek stranger of whom I asked my way to the bank. He took me there, and we found it closed, so changed money at his office. He then hailed a cab and informed me that he was going to shew me the country. He had a Napoleonic profile—the hundred days rather than the Directoire stage—and his English was founded on the three books on his office desk: *Business Phrases*, *A Summary of the British Constitution*, and a *Slang Dictionary*. It was very funny. We drove out and out into the country, flat and dusty with carub and acacia. We came to a Salt Lake with a beautiful range of hills reflected in it. I was getting slightly anxious, especially when he said the carriage could go no further, and took me along a path through the lonely sandy forest. It would have been delightful, only I was distracted from the beauties of nature by my doubts, and wondering whether this is how they always welcome strangers in Cyprus. At last I said firmly that I had gone far enough, and we returned, with nothing alarming by the way. Later on I discovered that my friend was the local tourist agent, and politeness his business in life. But even so, he carried it to an extreme point, for he would not let me pay for my cab, or my tea after, and even insisted on choosing my toothpaste for me at the chemist's: Cherry Blossom, he told me, "is fine, first-rate," and Cherry Blossom it had to be.

I don't know whether it was this excess of entertainment, or the sight of neat suburban things, schools, hospitals, clubs, and green railings; but I feel pleased to be in these shaggier lands again, where you need a police permit to go by train to the next village, and where it requires some discrimination to distinguish the police officer from your own ragged boatman.

To-morrow I hope to come into Arab-speaking country. It is very cold here. I live in my fur coat.

Your loving FREYA.

11. *To Miss C. A. Ker.*

S.S. *Diana*, OFF ALEXANDRETTA (ISKANDERUN). 8.12.27.
DEAREST CAR,

You must hear about this morning, for it was the last of your present, spent riotously and most successfully on a pilgrimage to Antioch all by myself (I being the only passenger now on board) with an Arab chauffeur and a boatman who refused to be shed at the landing stage. Great thrill to find my Arabic adequate for getting what I want, and even for a limited admiration of natural objects, though my adjectives are painfully monotonous.

We went high up; how high I don't know, but the Turkish wind came like a knife round the corners and there was ice in the ditches. We stopped at the first village to look at a khan—the proper sort with gloomy arches and animals tethered, and people stooping over fires in the small side chambers. The police came and looked at me benevolently; the boatman, who now fancied himself my personal bodyguard, handed cigarettes round to the village at large, and we went on, up the pass, through myrtle and oleander, and here and there a tree, past a long string of camels, a glorious sight against the sky; then down in loops and at a great rate, with the lake of Antioch lying as it were in the middle of a shallow saucer of marshy, fertile land with hill horizons on every side. Nothing moving in all the lonely country except black outlines of oxen ploughing. The villages are just clusters of low rooms thatched over, invisible at any distance. No trees, except here and there one solitary specimen.

It was astonishing after all this loneliness to find Antioch, with a ruined castle crag above and the muddy Orontes before it, swarming with life. Streets of red leather shoes; streets of carpenters, blacksmiths, weavers at their looms with the goat whose hair is being woven into saddlebags tethered to the doorpost. Every kind of costume and colour worn with every degree of casualness. The country-men who travel with their donkeys wrap up their heads so that the first impression is a population all suffering from toothache and nothing like the dignified turban of the *Arabian Nights*; but it is the *Arabian Nights* all the same.

I invited my two Arabs to coffee in the main street in the sun, our little cups of sweet sticky stuff on three chairs in front of us, and the goats and donkeys and vivid ragged garments all brushing by them. I very busy trying to eat an orange presented by the boatman, and after one prudish Western qualm, flinging the peel into the middle of the street with true Oriental spirit.

My Arabic was not good enough for enquiries about St. Paul. Besides, my chauffeur had said something about Armenians with so much vehemence that I thought he might perhaps dislike infidels altogether. I saw nothing of Christianity except one quiet square with the Greek church, very plain and whitewashed inside and out, and not remarkable except for the good proportion of its arches. All ruins; the medieval castle on its crags, the old walls almost unrecognizable in the marshy land; and a few Greek sarcophagi of marble; but the position in the centre of that rich country tells what a glorious place it must once have been.

The mosque was a place of peace. A little enclosed piazza of marble, mellowed by ages of sunlight, with four orange trees laden with fruit growing between the slabs of the pavement. Inside, the sun was streaming on to white walls, and arches just touched with green and yellow in a simple pattern, and the carpet floor blazing like a ruby. My chauffeur hesitated about taking me in; but my Arabic was too bad to understand objections; and there was no one inside but an old sheikh in a corner who woke up with smiles at my offering for the poor.

I am fairly flourishing; not good for mountains, but good enough I hope for Arab grammar.

Ever so much love from FREYA.

12. *To her Mother.*

s.s. *Diana*, TRIPOLI. 9.12.27.

DARLING B.,

An awful night last night. The wind comes howling down the empty funnels of these hills, and the poor *Diana* simply staggered under it. I followed its three separate melodies most of the night, the high piping in the rigging, the tramp of the engine working hard, and the slap of the seas which sent drops of cold water on to my face through the closed deck window. I have been feeling rather ill anyway the last few days and shall be glad of dry land.

Tripoli looks well from the sea. 'Rudel's castle stands above the middle of the town and the cedars of Lebanon are visible to the inward eye at the back. It was no good trying to get ashore as the captain refused to guarantee my coming out again and one has to be carried through breakers by the Arabs. There is a breakwater, of which we are on the lee side; but all passengers, and all the lighters full of Czechoslovakian sugar, and the poor drooping bullocks from our deck, have to go by the bad side where the douane is waiting for them through five or six lines of boiling foam. I suggested at lunch that two or three douaniers might walk across and wait for people on the easy side, but the two new passengers (who are Italo-French-Levantine officials) looked as if they thought me a Bolshevik. They say Jaffa is the worst of these roadsteads: I make a note to avoid it.

Did you have an eclipse of the moon last night? The captain called me, and the stars were like new pins and the moon smoky dull red, her left side just beginning to come to life again.

I should like to paint our cargo on the lower deck: a crowd of patient, unhappy sheep with drooping heads and long sad ears, and eleven black bullocks. The men, too, loading and unloading, with their baggy trousers and red tasselled tarbooshes, looking just like Sinbad the Sailor as I met him in the picture-book on my ninth birthday. Herbert gave him to me, and is probably responsible for my being here.

A British boat has anchored on the other side of the breakwater, and no one can go near it because of the high seas.

Your own FREYA.

The writer of these letters is now to spend three cold winter months at Brumana, a Syrian village on a slope of the Lebanon high above Beirut. She went with a recommendation from the well-known orientalist Sir Thomas Arnold, and her object in settling there was to gain a command of fluent Arabic. She had already received a grounding in this difficult tongue, first from an old Franciscan missionary friar at San Remo, then in 1926 from an Egyptian teacher in London, and finally in 1927 at the School of Oriental Studies.

13. *To Mrs. Jeyes.*

BRUMANA.   11 DEC. 27.

DARLING VIVA,

The last two days on board were really rather wretched. I was beginning to wonder what dispositions to make about my corpse when dry land and mountain air restored me. I now only have the ordinary pain, which I consider sufficient for one person's allowance, and rather hope a few months here will cure it, for the staple food is what they call *leban*, a kind of curds, and what could be more soothing?

My hostess, Mlle. Audi, is a gentle little thing with a sort of refined and faded youth still clinging to her, all alone with one maid in a little square stone house with whitewashed rooms, very clean and full of plants in pots. Stone-tiled floors and a stove in the sitting-room which, however, she says smokes in cold weather. "But then," she says, and points to a brass brazier on a tripod in the middle of the floor, "we sit round that, and it is delicious": and I can't help wondering whether it will be considered rude to sit in my fur coat.

Mlle. had a teacher all ready waiting called Salehmy, who is to teach me from 5.30 to 6.30 every day. Mrs. Fox at the Quaker Mission seems to have her doubts, but the head of their school is also going to see me, and between them they will no doubt hustle me along the paths of knowledge.

The time table here is almost monastic. Breakfast 8; lunch 12.30; tea 3.30; supper 6.30; bed 8.30.

Mrs. Fox has been here for years and followed Allenby's advance through Palestine with soup kitchens. She says the Turkish corruption is outshone by the present administration (I hope they don't censor letters here). The Maronites are the only people who wanted the French and they are now cooling off, and altogether this district is far worse off comparatively than it was before the war.

Your loving FREYA.

14. *To Miss Buddicom.*

BRUMANA. 14 Dec. 27.

MY DEAREST VENETIA,

I have taken my map and compass out this morning, and sat under a pine tree looking at Lebanon and thinking of you.

Brumana is a glorious village, a long ridge of neat stone houses with red hillside of pines drooping straight to Beirut and the sea, and Lebanon, a stony mass with narrow slits for valleys, rising very evenly to its snowy watershed on the south. It is all spotted with red-roofed prosperous bourgeois little hamlets, but even from here one can see where the civilized fringe ends, and when you join me we should get into lovely country inhabited by jackals and Druses where you may come round any lonely corner and see the flutes of Pan actually being played on. I saw this myself, and loved the sad sweet sound of them, and helped the owner to retrieve his chickens which, in the musical interval, had escaped off the back of his mule where all worldly goods here are carried.

If we go over this watershed (Lebanon) across the broad valley and along the fringe of Hermon by Rasheya (where much of the fighting was) to Damascus, it should take us ten fairly active days; without counting a couple of days at least for Hermon. I am a miserable being yet at hills, but should manage with a mule, and this route could, I believe, be managed at any time of year by a judicious arrangement of halts so as to avoid nights on the highest ridges. We should always be in fairly easy reach of civilization—very like Andorra with its grand hotels dotted at intervals and the good untouched country in between. Anyway I submit the plan, after looking at the country as well as I can from here and getting information from the local people. They all say it is too cold till May for sleeping out, but one can ask for hospitality from the village priest or sheikh.

Goodness knows how much of this impossible colloquial Arabic I shall be able to manage by the Spring! So far it seems difficult, but the greatest difficulty is to prevent the kind people here from practising all the European languages on me. I only wish I had not confessed to knowing French.

When I came here (four days ago) Mlle. Audi rather appalled me by saying that there was "quite a lot of Society in Brumana. Bible classes, Y.W.C.A., and Reunions for Improving one's Mind." So far this terrible vista has not filled in so far as I am concerned, except for a Quaker service on Sunday, hymns and sermon all in Arabic, and most improving though possibly not in the manner intended.

I long for a letter from you; and wonder when this will reach you. If anywhere near Xmas, it will bring my Xmas wishes, but the dearest love anyway and at any time.

Your loving FREYA.

15. *To Mrs. Jeyes.*

BRUMANA. 22.12.27.

MY DEAREST VIVA,

Nothing could have given me greater pleasure than to open your letter and find your picture inside. It was so nice to come upon it under my umbrella on this dreary day. I *have* to go out in any weather at least twice a day to keep warm, and the post is a good object when landscape is invisible in mountain deluge.

The Mission school gave its entertainment on Tuesday night and we all went. Such a funny mixture. One of the items will shew you what a jumble of scholars it is. They had eleven boys, each with one letter of the word BROTHERHOOD pinned on to his chest. They stood in a half circle, and each boy in his own language repeated a sentence to say that the world is one great family and his own nation a member thereof; it was English, French, Italian, Spanish, Portuguese, Greek, Hebrew, Armenian, Turkish Arabic, Egyptian Arabic, Syrian Arabic.

There was a sword-dance too, and that was fascinating. The two boys had real scimitars and targets and it seemed impossible they should not slash each other as the things whirled round their heads at terrific speed. I thought that one ought to be clapping time for them, and heard afterwards that they complained of the dispiriting effect of a perfectly silent audience.

Salehmy has been telling me that tigers used to inhabit the Ras el Meten valley where I was so happily wandering. I think this is a delusion, and that anyway he means panthers, and even so . . .! especially as he tells me such strange details about the domestic habits of the hyena. He says the hyena lures you into its cave, then *tickles* you till you die, so that it may eat you dead. (His French is poor, he may not quite know what he says.) "Why does one follow the hyena to its cave?" say I. "*C'est par la sympathie*," says Mr. Salehmy, very solemn in his effort to explain. He tells me however that Miss Cook is wrong in affirming that the hyena walks under our windows every night. What we hear are the jackals, careering in the valley with piercing little barks and shrieks that sound peculiarly evil.

Your loving FREYA.

16. *To her Mother*.

BRUMANA. 23 DEC. 27.

DARLING B.,

We had the first real winter's day here yesterday, a perfect deluge all day, and poor Mlle. in Beirut shopping.

The Stoneys wired they were motoring from Damascus, and arrived having done about 260 klm. in the rain, over two mountain ranges and round by Baalbek. I took rooms at the hotel for them, and found an oil stove too of which they probably did not value the uniqueness, and went with them to dine. It was cheerful to see them, and hear about their tour. Mrs. S. told me it was delightful in Jericho to see her husband (who farms his land in Ireland) and the Head of the Palestine Agriculture neglect all ruins of antiquity and, with every appearance of reverence, make for a low mound, which turned out to be a very special kind of manure.

They know the Government House people in Jerusalem and have offered me introductions both to the Plumers and the A.D.C., Capt. Drummond. The accounts they heard of Syria were much the same as I have here. Palestine, however, is to roll in wealth, the Dead Sea being all potash: so that something may be said even for Sodom and Gomorrah.

We had quite an exciting time finding the hotel in the dark and mud. I got into their car, which was already very full with various valises and one Armenian lady. She tried to assure us by saying that the local chauffeurs are so safe because always chosen among the married men; I amended to "*happily* married", which seemed to make her thoughtful.

We are going to tea to-day with missionaries from China. On Sunday two Syrian ladies to lunch. On Monday evening, entertainment at Mrs. Fox's. On Tuesday the Manassehs arrive, after having had their pockets picked and passports stolen in Paris—such an affair!

I begin to try my hand at sentences, but it is slow work. Rather pleasant however when I went to Mrs. Fox's and was asked how long I had been at it, to be told, when I said apologetically "two years," that "of course, that is *nothing* for Arabic." I get so tired of hearing it taken for granted that it is a language one can pick up like French.

I hope you have my letters now? They were such an effort to write when I was seasick, I cannot bear that you should not have them.

Your FREYA.

17. *To Miss Buddicom.*

BRUMANA. XMAS EVE. 1927.

MY DEAREST VENETIA,

It fills me with remorse to read your enthusiasm over the chance of seeing Baghdad—and me throwing cold water and being generally (as I do feel) most unsatisfactory. That wretched Prime Minister has not yet written, so it is still on the cards that I may not be able to go at all; in that case I shall linger as long as you like and we can find a Beduin camp outside Damascus or make our way to Rum if you can stay long enough. But I still hope for Baghdad and shall wait till the New Year and then jog His Excellency's memory.

In any case I feel that Baghdad is bad as a tramping centre; and I have discovered a new and conclusive reason to make it unsuitable and that is that the Iraqi Arabic is completely different again from the Syrian, so that it would mean starting with no knowledge of the language (for speaking purposes). As for this Syrian, I am distinctly hopeful and ought to know a little more than the Spanish which took us so happily on our Andorra trip. The difficulty is to get accustomed to a language which pronounces hardly any of its vowels. But I can now put three words together and understand them when spoken, and really feel rather pleased with myself.

I do hope, dear Venetia, you are thrilled over the Druse plan for I can't *bear* not to share these emotions. I long to have you for a look over the landscape and the map, one more alluring than the other. The essential is a good Druse guide, so as not to be drawn into religious troubles. I shall be able to get one through the Syrian doctor, who is away at present but returns next week. With enough Arabic to talk to our own guide, who will be able to make it clear that we are English and not French, there should be no trouble.

It is miserably cold. I have to take so many short walks just to get warmth into my body that the whole day has gone before I know it. The only time out of the twenty-four hours in which I am warm at all is the latter end of the night in my bed, or when the sun shines for a few hours into my room.

I must have some Stoic mixed with the Epicurean, for I can't help feeling pleased through all the discomfort at living as it were among real things; the sun not a mere ornament in the heavens, but something on which your day's happiness depends; and the Spring looked forward to with all the feelings which you find in the old writers before the days of comfortable houses.

You will like the building here. It is good square stone; neatly worked, and the Crusaders have left the pattern of their pointed arches, besides many carved pillars, which you see everywhere. It is pleasant after the ramshackle Turkish. *Inside*, the pointed windows and stone floors and general emptiness are Spartan. It is a funny mixture of primitive life and of French culture spread thin; I trot along beside Miss Audi with her high-heeled little shoes and shingled hair, and meet the tall shepherds striding down from the hills, with an air about them unfettered by anything Europe has brought.

It seems to me that much that the French have been doing here is thoroughly mischievous—setting up a small class of townsmen who will have all the actual business of governing to do with no training at all in common with the people they have to look after.

I am getting a fine knowledge of Syrian food for our mutual benefit. Very good too.

I have more to talk about. This writing is a clumsy business—all one really has to say left out. My love to you. I am glad you are in the world with me.

Your FREYA.

18. *To Mrs. Robertson.*

BRUMANA. XMAS DAY.

MY DEAREST MRS. ROBERTSON,

It is no good telling how often I have intended writing; that is always so feeble! But I do not want Xmas to pass without my dear and loving wishes.

This is really "between the desert and the sown," for

we are still among vines and mulberries and Beirut is a painfully Frankish town, and we go calling on each other in high heels and the Paris fashion last but one. But we look out to where the prosperous villages stop and the bare ridges go up to their watershed, and peasants come down from this country with gay beaded mules, sitting in baggy clothes on embroidered saddles, with a white cloth round their tarboosh if they happen to be Druses, and the rifle which the French have carefully eliminated obviously missing from their natural outfit.

I have been trying to think why it is all so fascinating. The country is not more beautiful than Italy, and these towns far less so, and here there is not much glamour of colour or costume. I have come to the conclusion that it is the feeling of a life not merely primitive—we have that in Italy—but genuinely wild. The Christian who has lived for centuries on the edge of massacre; and the Druse who no doubt still fills his winter evenings with tales of the Old Man of the Mountain—no amount of French education can cover this up. If I happen to be talking French as I stroll along the road with my landlady and catch a glance of hatred from some white turban passing by, it gives a feeling of the genuine original roughness of life which is worth the pilgrimage.

I have been received with great friendliness and the village is doing its best to teach me—only too pleased to find someone who has come neither to improve nor to rob, but with a genuine liking for their language.

You will be amused at my Christmas day. A Maronite mass at 8.30, the ceremonial like the Latin, only set to the *wildest* Arab music, with a fast fierce gaiety about it that made the oddest contrast with all memories of masses I have ever heard.

Then our Quaker meeting, where we sing Syrian hymns to the tune of "God Save the King," and rows of scholars from the Quaker school—Turks and Armenians side by side, Iraqis, Syrians, Greeks, Egyptians—listen politely while someone tells them that the World is really one harmonious family. This conglomeration of scholars is due to the motor car, and I am wondering whether Mr. Ford has not done something for the peace of the World after all.

After the meeting I came home with two Syrian Quakers and we had our Xmas dinner, and I listened for three hours, understanding about one word in a hundred. The colloquial is quite a different language from the classical, and I shall be pleased if my four months here teach me enough for the very simplest conversation. The trouble is that no amount of study can teach it, for everything *printed* is in the classical, and one can only learn the other by talking and listening.

The best of wishes, dear friend,

Your loving FREYA.

19. *To Mrs. Aidan Thompson.*

BRUMANA. 27 DEC. 27.

DEAREST P.,

Too bad to hear of jaundice. I do think we should be provided with a new body about the age of thirty or so when we have learnt to attend to it with consideration.

Mine bears up with decent amiability under the strain of Syria and Xmas combined, and I believe my bright pink nose is due not to my inner self at all, but to the unspeakable cold. I am really quite pleased that the poor old body is able to put up with so much discomfort without actually being any the worse, and the fact that if you are *never* warm you also never catch cold is being borne in upon me. Never mind! It is all marvellous just the same, and very like real life; and to-day I was really warm, for the sun shone in a sky bluer than anything but the best enamel and I went down the hill to try and find the water at the bottom. Every valley has a stream, I argued. But Lebanon has these deep clefts. You look across to a village quite close at hand, and it takes you a day to get there.

I talked to two woodcutters in turbans, the only beings in the solitude of rocks and pines. I have reached the interesting stage when I can ask my way and not possibly understand the answer.

You would be proud of your little friend if only you could hear what a multitude of adjectives expressive of the most exalted intelligence are lavished upon her—but as I know exactly how stupid I feel this does not disturb my equilibrium. I cannot manage more than three words at a time, and ungrammatical. My reading is all love or religion, the latter makes me feel at home with the sermons on Sundays and the former has no use for the present! I am working hard; three hours grammar and as much time after that as possible taking my landlady out for walks when I stammer on and insist on keeping her off perfectly easy French.

My teacher is a nice-looking young Syrian and comes every evening, fixes me with fiery eyes, and pours out rules of grammar which sound exactly as if a cat were spitting at me.

They are all Christian here—about six different sorts. The Druses come in from the hills, undistinguishable except by a white wrap round their heads, and a fiercer look about them. I am trying to induce Venetia to agree that our tramp should be through their country (quite safe, I think, if we have a Druse guide and if only I can speak a little). I am waiting to hear. Meanwhile I shall do no sightseeing but work and save up. I live here on 8s. 6d. a day including everything except postage stamps (my lessons are included).

Oh, my dear, you can hardly imagine what joy it is to be free all day long to do my own work; this alone was worth travelling across the world for. I sit in my little room and feel as if I were Queen of the Universe, and the fact that I have to get up and do exercises every half-hour to keep the circulation going makes no difference.

Such an appropriate picture over my desk, too: two polar bears surrounded by icebergs, eating what remains of a frozen boat with the legend "Man proposes, God disposes," unconscious Victorian irony.

The whole place is a most amusing mixture of Europe smeared thin on a whole depth of primitive life below. Even the landscape is like this with the perfect barbaric glory of its sunsets and its grand lines not laid out for peaceful friendly life, and then the neat villages built as tidily as toys. And you admire the little square houses and ask why so many of them are allowed to stand about roofless and windowless, and are told that these belonged to people who died of hunger during the war. And so it all is—life and death side by side with a suddenness which gives a good barbaric flavour.

Lovely silks, P. dear, I shall be tempted in Damascus, but shall have nothing left then.   But if you want me to get any for you, let me know.   The best are the gold woven gowns and the head shawls; I saw them in Antioch and hankered.

Otherwise there is nothing special here except the donkey harness, all "cockle shells and little bells," enough to make any donkey happy.

Shall we meet in Asolo next summer?

Your loving FREYA.

20.   *To Mrs. Ernest Barker.*

BRUMANA.   1ST JAN. 28.

MY DEAREST OLIVIA,

The very happiest of New Years to you and Ernest. I feel a worm for not writing before.

What am I to begin about now?   I think I shall just tell you my good day in the country last Thursday.   Such a good day it was, and I thought of you, and W.P., and many many happy things, walking along under the Lebanon pines, which looked for all the world like a gentleman's park, or perhaps like the less cultivated corners of the Garden of Eden with the wild outer world arranged as a background.

You should have seen the agitated circle of kind Syrians at Mlle. Audi's tea party the day before, begging me not to go.   Even the American mission lady assured me that strong men had been found half dead by the way; and finally a much-worried youth told me he would take his gun (for crows, not Druses) and see me as far as the bridge in the valley—my object being the village, which looks as if we could throw stones into its lap from this side.

It was very like Villatella country zigzagging down among myrtle, pine, and oleander and an incredible variety of thorns.   A good well-marked track, stonier than anything in Italy, however.   And, of course, a mule harnessed with beads (blue, against the evil eye) and cockleshells,

D

and a driver in red sash and turban, are more interesting than our sober people.

When I left my guide I began climbing the other side in the shadow. These valleys are so deep, the sun never gets at them I believe; you look up and see a rim of sunny villages about 2,000 feet over your head, and you walk in what looks like absolute solitude, until the voices of wood-cutters shouting out to each other the news of one solitary female wanderer make you feel painfully conspicuous— the sort of feeling I remember in the war when being suddenly focused by a searchlight.

When the track divided I was stunned, of course, and sat down to consider; then Providence provided a young man, who afterwards told me he had run over half a mile to see my interesting person at close quarters. He took me along through delicious woodland, his French and my Arabic being equally bad—till we finally came to his village and I had to be explained to the assembled relatives. I was invited into the house, and sat on a long divan admiring the beautiful clean whitewash and mats, and trying to answer questions about my clothes. The sister sat beside me with her arm round my neck, and the mother brought out their new dresses to show me. We then drank coffee, and I was asked to stay a month, or ten months, or a year, or at least a day; and finally I left with many kind words which I could not understand. My language does not yet run to sentences, and I get hopelessly tied up over the fifteen different ways of saying "good-bye" and "thank you".

After this adventure I found my way easily and got to the village (all Druse) by lunch time, and was given a second lunch at the mission, which is perched in an old Druse castle with all the hills of Lebanon round it. I wish I could tell you how beautiful it was. The ladies at the mission were particularly pleased that the only person so far to do the walk both ways should be a woman (the two Englishmen who attempted it having had to return ignominiously by car). I discovered the reason on my return home. Two Syrian boys accompanied me by a short track where anyone would get lost without a guide.

It was pleasant slipping down in the afternoon sun with

the scent of the pines and thyme all about me, the boys giving me scraps of Arab poetry or playing on their reed pipes, joined with wax just as Theocritus has it, and filling the wood with the wild sad sound as we walked along. "It needs a long breath to fill the pipes," they said.

In the crannies of the rock I found the first cyclamen.

I was home by four, and had not walked over six hours actually, but it is hard walking for I must have been up and down over 10,000 feet, much of it like stairways. My heart went like a hammer all night.

Tell Bernard I will write. My love to all meanwhile.

Your FREYA.

21. *To her Mother.*

BRUMANA. 1.1.28.

DARLING B.,

A Happy New Year to you! I was so pleased to get your letter when home from Beirut last night. I went to meet the Stoneys and their boat was not to come in till morning after all. I was disgusted, and haven't the energy to go again. It is an hour's hairpins, quite amusing with everyone jumbled into the cars: reminiscent of Mortola.

I had enough Arabic not to lunch in the hotel but found a ragout, sweet, and coffee for five francs (French) cooked for me over a primus stove in a lowdown little place without tablecloths. The gramophone was set going for my amusement.

I came back with a pleasant surprise for Mlle. She had lost one of her immense pearl (?) earrings, and I got her a new pair in Beirut, and she was very pleased and became pro-British in politics on the instant. I am her amusement and object in life just now. She invited the young French teacher to dine with my Syrian teacher, and we spent the evening arguing about Syria—he being one against three. He was finally told that it is only the English who *always* take an interest in the life and language of the countries they inhabit, which enormous untruth we both listened to in noncommittal silence.

It is all very like Italy in some ways. The Mediterranean

is one family. Of course Lebanon is quite different from Damascus and all beyond; but here I find that my Italian knowledge makes me at home in a way which is quite foreign to any of the English except Mme. Manasseh, who has really adopted the Syrian way of living.

But this is a sad people. Neither Arab nor European. They could not stand independently of Europe against the Moslems of the interior. And if they hang on to Europe they are made the tool of every disgusting politician. I believe there is nothing they can strive for with any hope of success. They are a fine-looking people too, magnificently built men, and women with eyes like stars. And hardy they must be, or they would be all dead. It seems a waste. Goodnight, dear B. Your own FREYA.

22. *To Miss Buddicom.*

BRUMANA. 4.1.28.

DEAREST VENETIA,

Did I answer your letter of the seventh? I know what you felt, for I have had the same thing—such a waste when one needs one's life for doing and feeling outside one's own poor body. I wonder will you be fit for the walking? Or should you have an extra mule all to yourself?

My nice Syrian doctor says he will find the Druse guide when the time comes. Meanwhile I have written to Baghdad and hope to hear.

About clothes—one light woollen and lots of warm things, and *shoes*: six hours over these stones reduces them to ribbons. I went to the next village, very pleased to see that my timing of three hours was absolutely accurate. I was four on the way, with an hour's rest. I really went to get my "eye in," and also to discover whether I could do it, and it seemed to work well enough. How good it will be when you are here. You will go into raptures over the country, and mid-March is the time for flowers.

I begin to attempt ambitious subjects like Doughty's travels in my efforts with Mlle. at lunch. I get plenty of practice. Every afternoon we pay a call, about two hours, and sit on a divan talking gossip interspersed with one of the sixteen formulas of politeness which I have collected so far. After a while a large tray is brought in with delicious sweetmeats, wine, tea, etc. We take a little of each (so bad for me) and say "May this continue" as we put down the cup. "May your life also continue" say our hosts. And then we leave.

I believe there is no feeling of class, at any rate in the country here. The division is religious, and as you see practically nothing of any religion but your own, you never have the unpleasantness of being surrounded by hostile people who are yet bound to mix up their lives with yours. Here, if I ask about someone in the village, Mlle. just says: "I don't know her; she is Greek Orthodox," or whatever it may be. Or "The Mohammedans in Beirut pronounce such a word differently"—like Benjamin and shibboleth! Think what a capacity for hatred it must mean to live for centuries in the same village and still feel like this about the next door neighbour. One can't help feeling sorry for the Mandatory who has to try and govern.

This is a miserable letter, all scraps; but it will never go unless I send it now.

Your loving FREYA.

23. *To her Mother.*

BRUMANA. 6.1.28.

DEAREST B.,

I have just got warm by going downstairs to see our neighbour make the flat sheets of bread I like so much. She sits on the floor with a round flattish cushion on one knee and smooths the balls of dough out on a board with her palms and fingers till they are about the size of a plate. Then she throws them with a very neat quick movement first over one forearm, then over the other. Her arms are very brown, tattooed and with twisted gold bracelets. The round of dough grows and grows miraculously till it is about two-and-a-half feet across and almost transparent. She then tosses it on to her cushion, arranges the edges so as to make it as nearly round as possible, and throws it all in one movement, so as not to crease it, on to a little metal dome which is on the floor and has a few sticks and pine needles burning underneath it. In one minute the whole thing is cooked, and if the fire is well distributed, is nice and crisp all over, and very good. And it has the advantage of being good to eat for a week.

While I sat there, the Greek Orthodox priest came and blessed us all with his little pail of water and brush of myrtle twigs. Yesterday we had the blessed bread sent us, a sort of X-bun flavoured with spices, which ought to have had a more soothing effect on my inside than it seems to have managed.

My Syrian won't let me pay for my school books because he says he is so pleased I am learning his language.

The Manassehs have come. He is a dear, like a benevolent child, and so like the Colonello in expression, I have to love him only for that. There are two sets here. Those who are all for being Anglicised, and the Manassehs belong to these; and those who are more for Arabic. And of course I am more popular with the latter.

H's letter just come. Tell him he shall have my next, for he deserves it more than my neglectful parent.

Your own FREYA.

24. *To Mrs. Jeyes.*

BRUMANA. 7.1.28.

DEAREST VIVA,

I was interested in the news of Ja'far Pasha, for he has not written a word (being so busy with treaties) and I do not know whether I am to go to Baghdad or not at the end of March. The other alternative is the desert beyond Damascus. I have an introduction (so to speak) for some of the tame Beduins, but am still in hopes that the more comfortable palace may be available.

Some day, when I can get away and if I am still alive, I must come for a whole year and get the language into my bones. I shall not be happy till I can *think* in Arabic.

So far no one understands me except Mlle., who is so like Miss Matty that I sometimes feel I am wearing a crinoline myself here. She is not pretty, but has dainty little hands and feet and clothes, and inexpressibly refined manners; and is always fluttering with emotions, which she lives on, I believe, for she never seems to eat. She has refined little flirtations (if so barbarous a word may be used for it) with the young French teacher, who is a Communist with a cherubic expression and large placid hands, from somewhere near Beaune. He was invited here for the evening, and kept us up till 10.30, much to Miss Rose's annoyance, who fears that such dissipation will be talked about among the neighbours.

I do envy you your mild weather. But that is all I hanker for, and I am not lonely—not more than one is anywhere in this box of a life. And happy to be at my own work.

There is a nice woman here named Faridi who taught T. E. Lawrence Arabic down at Jubeil, when he was wandering among the old Syrian forts on his first coming East. I believe she is one of the few women he ever writes to—not beautiful but with a good intelligent rough face and manner—and very kind to me since, as she said: "You are one of us!"

I feel so good. Every evening a prayer meeting for the first week in the year. It is mostly in Arabic. I can now recognize psalms and the names of most of the ordinary virtues; but whether these will be useful among the Druses remains to be seen.

Ever so much love from FREYA.

25. *To her Father in Canada.*

BRUMANA. 14.1.28.

DEAREST PIPS,

I don't know, but I rather think I have been more than a week without writing. The days all go so quickly, one very like another, and one doesn't notice. It was very nice to look down through the field-glasses two days ago and see three big steamers in harbour, 2,300 feet below, and then sit expecting letters: and sure enough there was a fat batch, and your good note.

It is good to feel you getting on.   It is bound to be long
—not as long as my unspeakable complications, if that is
any comfort, which of course it isn't.   It will mean being
careful.   I have also had to get accustomed to the feeling
that all the pleasant world may suddenly and at any
moment come to a stop as far as I am concerned—and it
doesn't seem to spoil things, does it?   Rather gives them
a peculiar valuable flavour; a kind of glorified gambling
feeling—and I hope we may have this for many years.
What I resent are days of pain and stupidity one has to
put up with, and I am glad you are pretty well out of
these.   I have made up my mind that if ever I get really
ill again I shall try to come out here, live on their sour
milk, and be invisible to my friends till the business is well
over.

I had a good walk to-day, up the valley to the next
village and saw fine country to explore, but everything is
much further away than you would think.

I have been enquiring about a small donkey harness
for the children—trimmed with shells and yellow and red
tassels, and a collar of blue beads against the evil eye.   The
saddles are huge affairs of wood covered with ornamental
carpet, the front, rather like the old feudal saddles, very
much raised, all studded with nails on leather.   There
are lots of cars here, but only for passengers, and all the
transport seems to be mule or donkey, and if anyone has
potatoes, or cabbages, or oranges to sell, he just puts
them on his animal and goes crying them through the
villages.

Your own FREYA.

26.   To Mrs. Herbert Olivier.

BRUMANA.   14.1.28.

MY DEAR MARGARET,

It is a disadvantage that one cannot be in two
places at once.   I shall not be home till well into June,
and even this seems sadly early.   The East is getting a firm
grip.   What it is I don't know: not beauty, not poetry,
none of the usual things.   This place is a grand scene with

all the details neglected. Of course it is not the genuine
Orient, only the semi-European fringe full of French ideas
second-hand and second-rate, and European clothes and
furniture peculiarly unadapted to the casual Eastern
silhouette. And yet I feel I want to spend years at it—
not here, but further inland, where I hope to go as soon
as I get enough Arabic for the absolutely necessary amount
of conversation.

The village is kind, at least the Christian part, for we
all live in separate compartments and have little to do
with such people as Druse or Greek Orthodox, though
we may live next door. My landlady speaks of the Druses
as Napoleon used to be spoken of to naughty children in
England. Even the languages are different and you will
be told that the Mohammedans pronounce "a" in a
way of their own just as the Druse women wear a
white veil.

Everyone here is much interested in my Arabic. It
seems I am the first to come and learn it *for pleasure*
and this gives great satisfaction not unmixed with
wonder.

I do so agree with what you say about the interest of
people; they are more than scenery, or art, or any of our
fashions. But why limit it to any particular bit of the
world? I find them just as human here as anywhere else:
and one great interest in such a different civilization is
that it gives you a sudden fresh view of your own; the
nearest in fact to getting out of the world and examining
it as an object. The only people I don't care to study
are the uncivilized—African, or American. Here it is
too much, not too little, civilization that is the trouble.
That, and an incapacity for forgetting. Mlle. Audi talks
of iniquities of Druse governors two hundred years ago as
if they had just happened. It is amazing to see all the
primitive feelings coming through the refined convent
breeding.

I have good news of my father. Did I tell you he
had been ill? I shall have to go out next autumn but
hope it may be combined with London and a sight
of you.

Your affectionate FREYA.

27. *To her Mother*

BRUMANA. 14.1.28.

DARLING B.,

Your letter and chocolates just come—thanks ever
so; I am so glad of both. Galetti in the warmth of his
feelings put a value of L.60, which made me pay a great
deal this end, but I am very glad to have something to
give people here. They say the douane is 33 per cent
from *France*!—one of the many things that are wrong.

There is a rumour going round that Italy will take over
Syria: I don't believe there is even one Syrian who desires
it, and it is rather too bad to see the Powers at work bandy-
ing people about in this unprincipled way. If Italy gets
it, it will not be long before she is sorry! It is a
poor country, and will never give much return, and I
should think as difficult to govern as any country in the
world.

A little less cold these days and a feeling of Spring in the
air: I took a long walk and got beautifully warm, but not
yet feeling very well. *Much* better here than in most
places, however—good water, healthy air and people, and
Mlle. simply living for my food. I have the same sort of
happiness as a man with a devoted and domestic wife, and
sympathize with his contentment. Poor Mlle! We went
to tea yesterday and there were lots of people, and Miss
C. (whose manners are casual and bad) didn't say either
good-day or good-bye: and Mlle. was quivering like one
of your small earthquakes all the way home. What a lot
of time and energy we save by having so few feelings!

I have finished my first grammar book and am considered a Perfect Prodigy. It is practically learning a
new language, and I hear with pleasure that the new
Persian scholar at the school has to be spoken to in purest
classical or he does not understand a word.

I have been to see the embroidery school—hybrid things,
spoilt by Miss C's Kensington touch. Some beautiful old
things. I think, however, I shall devote myself to glass
from the tombs; it is such wonderful colour. What do you

say? Or shall I spend all my money on X-raying my anatomy before I go among the Druses?

Such fun at the meeting on Sunday. I thought the Arabic hymn sounded strangely familiar, and it suddenly dawned on me that we were singing it to the tune of God Save the King. It struck me as comic to make the benighted Syrian sing our own National Anthem when he wants to offer up a special prayer for Syria.

Dear love to H. and a kiss to you from FREYA.

28. *To Miss Buddicom in India.*

BRUMANA. 18.1.28.

DEAREST VENETIA,

I was just wondering when your letter of the 4th came—and I take it you have got mine, telling you all about this country. It grows on me more and more, even though I suffer from perpetual chills. But March should be good, and full of flowers.

It breaks my heart to think you will see Damascus before we walk in with our mules, and I am worried to think of the long air-voyage for you. I believe it is the least uncomfortable way overland, however.

You must make your plans on the assumption that I go to Baghdad end of March, though I do not really know, and have just heard that my man is Minister no longer, which explains the delay. I hope it is no longer the fashion to put them in sacks and drown them at the end of office, just before I pay my visit.

We are having most appalling weather. I see it pouring with the comfortable feeling that it is best to get it over now; and it makes it easier to sit over the pages of grammar if there is not all loveliness outside waiting to be explored.

What fun we shall have buying coloured saddle-bags! Don't, don't linger in Damascus. You will see it from a horrid European hotel and it will be all wrong.

I've come to the conclusion I don't like missions. I don't believe they are in any real touch with the people here, and feel they could have done so much better by just existing as a Christian school with no pretension to improve the heathen. It is extraordinary to see how little they manage to share the life of the place. I believe I am considered eccentric for preferring the Syrians to these little Englands outside England which might just as well be within reach of the District Railway so far as any Eastern influence upon them goes. They will tell you how to get silk scarves, or Armenian servants, or British colony gossip (I suppose there are exceptions, but these also avoid the tea parties, I imagine). The Syrians are charmed to find that anyone is genuinely interested in their language and them. I feel that the real way to be a missionary is to come and *learn*.

I wait to hear when to expect you. Shall I fetch you in Damascus with a car from here? It will be cheaper and I shall have the joy of consulting about our route as we drive through the country.

I envy you the night in the jungle.

Your FREYA.

29. *To Herbert Young.*

BRUMANA. 19.1.28.

DEAREST HERBERT,

I think you really deserve the next letter, for your two gave me so much pleasure, and my wicked mother does neglect me.

I wonder what you would have thought of the Beduin music yesterday. I went in the doctor's car to help at their Sanatorium Xmas tree. Deluges very like Mortola, and the blankets, which had been put up as screens on the open loggia, billowing about in a hurricane. The three Beduins, one a little girl of about ten, invited themselves in, very draggled and ragged, and sat on the floor with their instrument. It was their own make, a tin oil-can with a stick poked through and a peg stuck into the stick with a horse hair string drawn taut over a piece of wood by way of bridge. The bow was a crooked stick with another horse hair, and the music had a weird monotonous melancholy as if the desert winds had wailed for centuries and taught its secret tunes. We had a great time afterwards keeping the loot from these people, who grabbed all within reach. And then we had to keep the patients from pillaging the Xmas tree, and finally returned wet through and weary.

I am so tired of the deluge. Mlle. took pity on me and offered a hot bath. But it is not of the kind one gets right into, so that the water, nearly boiling over bits of me, and the rest of me in Arctic regions, made me feel like those ices with the hot chocolate sauce poured over them. I felt it was a pleasure too *mixed* to be repeated.

Your loving FREYA.

30. *To her Father.*

BRUMANA. 21.1.28.

DEAREST PIPS,

I have just discovered that the little drawing-room window high up near the ceiling has no glass to it, so perhaps that explains why the stove has so little influence! It is like Paradise when I sometimes go and sit by one of the English fires, but I have evolved quite an elaborate system of self-protection now, and also—we really are going towards the Spring. I remember there is an ode of Horace beginning "*Non semper imbres*" or some such, which expresses my feelings.

I have been hearing stories of Druse massacres in 1860. It seems that an English doctor and his wife happened to be travelling in these seas at that time. He was ill, and put ashore and died in Beirut just when the trouble occurred, and his wife in her widowhood was touched by the sight of Druse widows and children pouring down into the town without food or shelter. She and the British Consul did all they could for them, and afterwards when she went home, she interested her brother in the business and they came out and started the British missions here. The Druses have never forgotten, and love us as much as they hate the French (and that is a good deal). I am told that when V. and I go about in their villages we shall find them very friendly. Last year, however, one could not go even to the next village with safety, and Mr. Oliver, who runs the mission at Ras el Meten across the valley and is adored in all the countryside, had to drive with a Union Jack on his car as the habit was to shoot first and ask after.

Dearest Pips, bless you, I hope you are all right. I wish you were nearer, with no Atlantic in the way. India seems no way off: Venetia is to fly over in four days.

Your FREYA.

31.　*To her Mother.*

BRUMANA. 21.1.28.

DEAREST B.,

I went yesterday to call on Mrs. Fox. I am so lucky in meeting people all anxious to help and befriend. Mrs. F. is giving me letters to an elderly missionary lady in Damascus who will, I hope, find V. and me a room instead of going to the hotel. Mrs. F. says that if we go into the Druse country, the trouble will be with the French, who will take us for spies. I wonder if you could ask Giustino to procure a letter from someone at the Embassy to say we are innocuous?

I suppose we shall be going some time in March, and will let you know where to send my summer things. So far clothes have been right, and a source of interest in the village. Mr. Chamoun, who is the Syrian headmaster and the most intelligent person here, confided to Mlle., after thinking it over for some weeks, that he thought I *could not* be intending to be a missionary. Perspicacious man! *What* I am, and why learning Arabic, is a mystery. I can't help them in the matter. If I say I do it for pleasure, there is a look of such incredulity that I begin to feel as self-conscious about it as if I were telling the most blatant lie.

Your own FREYA.

32.　*To Mrs. Jeyes.*

BRUMANA. 22.1.28.

MY DEAREST VIVA,

It is good to hear that your various breakages and damages are really mending—mended I hope by now. I have your letter, and am grateful to think of warmth and comfort on the way! Just now there is a spasm of mildness, but I am told it is quite a mistake to think the worst is over, and that the elders of the village usually, if they are wise, go to bed in February and reappear in March. I might do likewise, but I am sure Salehmy would refuse to give lessons at my bedside like the Egyptian: he is nothing if not a most decorous young man. I can only hope his really beautiful eyes are not completely wasted: in fact I don't think they are. He comes twice a week in the evening after supper and then, after the lesson, we tell our fortunes with a crystal ball I once bought at a Glasgow fair and had the lucky idea of bringing with me. And then we play cards! You have two packs, one in a jumble in the middle of the table and the other held by one of the players who turns the cards over slowly: you all try to draw out the similar card from the table pack as fast as you can, using only your little finger. This simple game, which rouses all one's worst fighting instincts, was taught me in Rhodes, and is a great success. It has slightly redeemed my reputation after a dismal show the other night when they worried me into reciting a French poem. You can imagine my feelings—the whole room swimming and I nearly choked with my own heartbeats. I am not meant for a public sort of life!

I have been missing all sorts of interesting stories about Lawrence. We took tea at his friend Faridi's house, and the Arabic was beyond me, all except the description of how he arrived at Jubeil, very dilapidated after three months travelling with only twenty Arabic words and one suit of clothes; and how he stayed there three months. Faridi then wrote him out a copybook full of all the words he could want to help him on his way. After he had been in the desert a long time, he came back one day with his Beduin. Faridi was told that a gentleman wanted her who could talk good Arabic which no one was able to understand. She told me that in fact she could not make out a word at first—such is this impossible language. The people who come here to school from Iraq take two months or so to know what the village is saying.

I went this morning to the Greek Catholic mass. The

churches are like square boxes with a small hole in the roof for the bell and cupola over it. When I got inside I was surprised to find a beautiful old carved apse, all very dilapidated and poor. There were few here of this variety of religion, and the church has been unlucky besides; its altar was demolished by lightning two years successively, which must be discouraging for the faithful. The service was a family affair, rather pathetic. The mustard-yellow check overcoats of the two young men who did the singing spoilt the general effect. The mixture of absurdity and solemnity, reverence and triviality, one feels so strongly in all these Christian sects. They have existed just on the edge · of massacre for centuries, and this does give a certain dignity to their absurd differences—even to my fat friend the priest from Aleppo.

To-day I was stopped in the road by the owner of the public house, who told me that till I came he had never liked a European lady! This had to be translated, being, I am happy to say, out of my usual repertory, and I was rather uncertain which of my sixteen polite formulas to use in reply! Your loving FREYA.

33. *To Miss C. A. Ker.*

BRUMANA. 26.1.28.

DEAR CAR,

You are fairy godmother. Such a wonderful birthday present! I shall take it down to Beirut next week and promptly fall into every temptation I can find. What fun! I say Thank You only once, but shall think it often while wealth trickles through my fingers.

Some of it shall be devoted to a comfortable donkey. Venetia comes in March and I mean to get her to look at Druses with me, as many of them as still live this side of Damascus since the French bombing. I think it would be about a fortnight's march, taking it easy and sleeping in villages, and I was just thinking how much more comfortable it would be if I could afford half a donkey to fall back on when tired, and behold, here the creature is—or as good as, for it is just finance that does it.

I am longing to try my Arabic with no other languages about. The hill talk is nearer the classical and altogether pleasanter than this untidy town talk. The hill people are the right sort wherever they may be.

I went yesterday for a long cross-country exploration with lunch in my pocket—quite unnecessary for everyone offers food as one goes and what I actually ate turned out to be delicious—dried figs wrapped in the local bread (which is thin like sheets of coarse brown paper) and pulled by a gentleman by the wayside from somewhere in the region of his tummy, inside his big red sash—inside everything he had on, I rather suspect. However, it was all wrapped up in a clean white handkerchief and tasted remarkably good. I gave chocolate in return.

He found me in the wilderness, for I took a short cut and, after losing myself among stones and thorns—stonier and thornier than any I know—I was clever and found a wood-cutters' path. There I met the man and was told that no lady had ever been seen here before, and was I married? This is always the first and most interesting question; I suppose they think a husband should keep me safely at home.

It was good walking in the solitude with the cyclamen and blue anemones blossoming all to themselves in little glades. The valleys go up steep as stairs from their river beds till you reach the first shelf: then up from shelf to shelf of good wide, level ground, till you find mulberry patches, and vines and villages on the third or fourth ledge where the sun can shine all day. There are no people down below except wood-cutters and charcoal burners. Now and then in the stillness you hear their axes and look and look till something gleams and moves among the tufts of trees and grey rocks. I don't believe even the winds get down into these deep valleys. One feels as if one were surprising a secret as one goes down—and it is almost as pleasant to come up again and meet the first cows or donkeys browsing about on the other side.

Your loving FREYA.

E

34. *To Mrs Aidan Thompson.*

BRUMANA. 26.1.28.

DEAREST P.,

It was good to have a proper letter to browse over and to hear all the news. I am slightly troubled at the thought of his being so charming, for it will be depressing to have *no* unmarried friends left, and I have just come to the conclusion that I simply can't bear to part with my own charming and amusing life while I am well to enjoy it—and I can hardly offer it even to the most undeserving husband when I am curled in cramps (which however has ceased to be since the cold stopped). So what am I to do while you are behaving like the Queen of Spain, and me left with no one to talk to?

How I do dislike people with Moral Aims. Everyone asks me why I learn Arabic, and when I say I just like it, they looked shocked and incredulous. Not the Syrians. They all love me, and hand me round as an interesting and amusing specimen whose clothes are far more absorbing than what the mission usually provides. I must try to get accustomed to feeling conspicuous, for it will get worse and worse if Venetia and I go into the hills.

Yesterday, as I came from a walk through a little group of houses, I was invited in (they always do this). I was glad of the rest, too. The rooms were beautifully clean; stone floors and straw mats. In one corner a new yellow and white quilt and a head all wrapped in bandages (I thought). The lady of the house went up and shook the protesting head from its sleep. I couldn't tell whether it was a man or a woman, but asked whether it was wounded.

"Oh no," said the lady, much surprised, "she is the mother of a baby," and there in the cradle, so covered that not a breath of air could touch her, was a two-day-old baby girl. "Another one here," said the grandmother, lifting a far corner of the quilt and rolling out a child. "And another here," turning over what seemed to be a small bolster. I sat contemplating from the divan, feeling

as one does in the presence of the conjurer who manufac-
tures rabbits, and not knowing what to say. Three girls
one on top of another is a real calamity to a poor young
wife. "You must be happy with your 'bint'," says I
inadequately at last. "You can take one away with you,"
says the mother, suddenly arousing herself to animation.

They were pleasant people—very like the sort whose
soup we ate at Pedriola. They asked me to stay the night
(under the quilt, I suppose), and made me go up to the
edge of the mattress on the floor so that the young wife
might slowly take me in from the top of my hat to my
shoes. She did this in silence, very solemnly: "Sweet,"
she then murmured with a sigh, and went to sleep again,
and I left with grandmother's blessings.

In the afternoons I go visiting with Mlle. and try to
follow what seems one unbroken stream of conversation
with no divisions for words in it.

I have found you a nice present: a blue glass bracelet from
one of the old tombs at Byblos. I am going to buy it next
week, and one for myself too so that I may bear to part with
the twin! I looked at them the last time but was too poor;
but now I have the delightful feeling of riches, thanks to
Car's birthday present, which is to be turned all to delights.

Dear P., not September. Couldn't you manage July
in Asolo? Oh do.   Your loving FREYA.

35. *To her Father in Canada.*

BRUMANA. 27.1.28.

DEAREST PIPS,

I have your card, and am sorry to hear of such cold.
It will be good when the warm weather begins. We go
nowhere near zero here, but the coldness indoors makes
up for what is wanting in the elements. When there is a
patch of sunlight all is well, and I move myself, my chair,
and grammar round my bedroom all morning from east
to west in harmony with the sun.

I wish you had been walking with me two days ago: I
was thinking of you all the time, for it was good exploring,
just seeing the objective and making up your mind where

the path might be to take you to it. I think you taught me to be quite fairly good at path-finding. Do you remember coming down on Casteldelfino in the mist? Here is clear enough weather; the obstacle is thorns. The gospel parables become vivid whenever one steps among them, and the only short cuts are wood-cutters' tracks which, once lost, are almost impossible to find again, and they are almost invisible even when you are on them. The people are full of friendliness and curiosity. I can't yet speak enough to get the best out of them, but they are very like our mountain people, even more hospitable, and with the same good manners, dignified and with no sense of inequality. None of the unpleasant class feeling here except as a European import from the towns.

There have been a good many robberies lately. Four turkeys from our next door neighbour. Now a poor tailor who has had all he owned in the world carried off in the night. The Armenians are suspected "at a venture." No one likes them. They say "The Armenian drinks and then throws stones into the well." But there doesn't seem to be any evidence in this case. Now the police have found a button, and hope to trace the thief. Meanwhile a little factory has been robbed, and people are reported to be wandering about in motors at night, knocking at the doors of houses where there are lonely women, and then raiding them with their heads wrapped up and only their eyes showing—a horrid shock. Mlle. begs me to sleep with my window on to the road closed, as otherwise the chair which is propped against the front door every night has no *raison d'être*. I should hate to see a white head with nothing but eyes climbing over the balustrade, so have had to comply. Do keep well, dearest Pips. I wish the winter were over and me going out already. Must I book a passage long before?   Your own FREYA.

36. *To Mrs. Jeyes.*

BRUMANA. 30.1.28.

DARLING VIVA,

I have been warm, as far as my feet go, for the first time this winter, and all thanks to you. I can't tell you what grateful thoughts I send. It is really a *comfort*, besides the fact that everyone thinks my slippers the very latest thing for drawing-room wear. I have never been anywhere where it is more fun to have clothes: everyone is so interested in them, and if I put on a fresh hat on Sunday mornings, it is with the agreeable certainty that it is going to give pleasure to the whole congregation.

When there is anything new, the etiquette is to shew it to all your visitors. To-day we paid a morning call to some people near by and were shewn, first, the new coat and shawl sent from sons in America; and next, the new W.C. We went in procession, husband, wife, daughter, son-in-law, and the chain was pulled with solemn pride—only no waterworks followed. I rummaged among my adjectives for something suitable, and finally brought out "healthy" with what I consider creditable discrimination.

I have been discussing Missions with my Quaker friend, Mr. Chamoun, the Syrian headmaster. He is clever and charming. He asked me to a Committee of the "Seekers after Truth" at Mrs. Davidson's. I told him I am a seeker after truth, but not in committees, and we began to talk. He says that the Missions, instead of being centres to produce native missionaries, manage to discourage every native development, and end by being just surrounded by a small clique of their own with no outside influence at all—very much what Lawrence has to say about the British officials. One certainly feels here that the missionary mountain is very expensive for the production of its mole. And they are all such good painstaking people: just unimaginative, the trouble at the root of most misunderstandings.

Did you know that camels in the evening bring bad luck? Eight of them came padding past our door at dusk as we came up the steps; rolling along like waves in the half light. They have a very soft footfall, as if they were treading on dust. I don't think it is only my romantic mind that clothes them with mystery. Mlle. told me of the ill omen and was reluctant even to pause and watch as they rolled by. We called to the Beduin (or she did) to ask whence they came, and were told Zahle, which is near the ridge we look at. I hope Venetia and I may get into their country.

I find that Salehmy has been spreading wild undeserved descriptions of my brilliant Arabic and altogether unprecedented intelligence! It is all because I remember his dull grammar, of which he makes me learn two pages a day by heart; and also, I imagine, because the feminine standard is low. It is horrid to be looked upon as a Prodigy when one isn't, and to have the truth when I tell it all put down to modesty.

Mlle. told me to-day how she watched the Allies entering Beirut from her little balcony up here. There were two "Fregates," or three (she can't remember) : one was British, and the other French. The French flew an enormous flag, and the British waited to let her pass first into the harbour, right up against the quay: and Mlle., looking through her glasses, realized that it was to be France in Syria after all.

I am walking well now. In and out of five villages, and twice up and down the valley without complaining. It was a good five and a half hours, all sunshine and solitude with interludes of villages full of interest and hospitality. It is remarkable that not even the British here seem to walk, and they talk of anything across the valley as if quite out of reach of the human feet. Not only that, but my going alone seems to strike them as peculiar, though how to be avoided when there is no one to go with isn't clear.

Your loving FREYA.

37. *To her Mother.*

BRUMANA. 2.2.28.

DARLING B.,

Your smiling face is on my writing table—such a lovely present. Thanks so much, dear B. It was a beautiful birthday surprise.

I am just revelling in the pleasantness of having spent all I possess—and I do nothing but remember fresh people who would like presents. We went to the weaving village. Alas, they get their silks from Europe now, though mulberries are the chief crop here. They send the good yellow silk to France, and get the artificial stuff in exchange.

We spent a morning in Beirut choosing a gramophone, and Mlle. now spends her time listening to foxtrots. The missions disapprove, but here is Mr. Chamoun, head of the school, with five children dancing away, and Mlle. starting the wicked practice in her own house. And it will be put down to me, who had nothing to do with it.

I called on Mrs. Satow. It was rather nice to find one-self in an English drawing-room unpervaded by prayer. She hadn't a good word for missions: told me they were mischievous, giving an education completely unsuited to the country, arrogant and narrow minded. She herself is a well-bred woman, looking as if the East had been a little too much for the surface of her temper, but pleasant under-neath. She had little good to say of the Syrians: the rich beneath contempt. During the war, she told me, the Turks gave enough grain to keep everyone alive—just— and the rich Syrians kept it in their cellars and doled it out at high prices, mixed with gravel which used to be sold openly for this purpose in great heaps in the bazaars. (I couldn't help thinking that Piedmont hadn't been so very much better, but didn't say so.)

The School has started evening classes for the village, much to the annoyance of poor Salehmy, whose only time for improving his own mind was the evening. He came yesterday, filled with annoyance and amusement because, instead of a rise in salary or an hour off in the daytime, Mr. Fox had merely added a special prayer on behalf of the evening teachers. All these rifts in the lute are coming to light as I am getting adopted by the Syrians!

We have had the Manasseh girls. They are quite pretty, and gay—only they *never* polish their shoes, or brush their hats, or hide any safety-pins: which just shews that they really are not meant for European clothes.

My dear love. Thanks for all the gossip.

Your FREYA.

38. *To Mrs. Ernest Barker.*

BRUMANA. 2.2.28.

DEAREST OLIVIA,

      The rain has set in now, coinciding rather happily
with a blister on my foot: and the two combined keep
me at grammar. It is quite amusing to get at it in the
tortuous Eastern way.

      My poor Syrian gets so cross because I will ask questions,
He has never done such a thing in his life, I am sure,
and yesterday when I gave him a pencil and asked him to
correct something in the printed book, he looked as if
Authority were sliding downhill before his very eyes. I
am his first European pupil (feminine), and I believe
inspire the pleasant pain that a hard scrubbing gives.

      I haven't been anywhere except for two good days in
the country and a drive to the Dog River—two walls of
rock going up in grey tiers, a Roman aqueduct, and black
goats on the narrow ledges, and the old writings of the
Conquerors where the rocks open out to the sea. We
deciphered Marcus Aurelius, being good Roman prose,
and left Saladin's rhymes as too difficult. A solitary
asphodel, the only one yet out, was blossoming like an
Elysian symbol below Sennacherib's tablet.

      The new gramophone is going for all it is worth and
Mlle. bending over it trying to catch the words of an
improper French song she bought by mistake. Now whom
does that remind you of ?

                              Your affectionate FREYA.

39. *To her Father.*

BRUMANA. 2.2.28.

DEAREST PIPS,

      When I tell you that I got a small electric shock
last night from my own silk petticoat as I was slipping it
over my head, I hope you will not think I am inventing.
It was really like an explosion of pinpricks. It has been
hot these two days: such a pleasure: the sea condensing into

steam and then clouds, and now the rain has come and it is pouring steadily. It appears that after such a repertoire one must always expect hail. I am sorry for the misguided almond trees with white blossoms. The anemones I believe behave like lesser celandines and shut themselves up: there are carpets of them under the pines near Beirut.

My master Salehmy and I are going through a regular minuet of politenesses. First he sent me two *beccaccie* (is that snipe?)—very good too. Then I invited him for a picnic with the Manassehs and Mlle. Now he is giving a soirée to let me hear Arabic music.

The picnic was a success. We zigzagged down to the plain feeling rather like an aeroplane on the verge of looping the loop, and ran along between sea and banana groves till we reached the pass of the conquering armies. They have all been along there. As a pass it is rather disappointing—not a very high defile, but steep and made of grey rock uncompromising enough, and the conquerors have left their stories in tablets that look small beside the flowing river and so much more ancient passage of Time. The Assyrians, bearded kings, have noses very like some of the present inhabitants. Then down through illegible Greek to M. Aurelius, Saladin, Napoleon and the British. All these very sober and plain. It only remained for the peculiar bad taste of the French to put the largest inscription of all with bronze and helmets and palms—apparently for chasing poor King Feisul out of Damascus. I couldn't help remarking on it to Salehmy, who, being Maronite and pro-French, looked pained.

We finished the day by going to the one Lebanon village where they weave: three little looms in a shed, and a shop over the way where the splendour of the East unrolls in dressing-gowns and terrible cushion covers. They are bad as soon as they leave the old Byzantine designs of cypresses and roses. We asked how they came to evolve the hideous European designs, and were told that "we know the leaves are green and the rest is easy." It was fun helping Salehmy to choose a wine-coloured gown with gold pyramids down its back to wear at parties.

It is good to think of Spring, and then Summer.

Your own FREYA.

40. *To her Mother.*

BRUMANA. 5.2.28.

DARLING B.,

I dined last night with the Fox's, and Miss Harvey, the secretary, and Mr. Edmunds, who teaches mathematics; and it turned out that Mr. Fox comes from Taunton and is a far removed cousin of ours in Torquay. Awful shock to find relatives in Syria! Mrs. Manasseh's cousin lives next door to the Whibleys: altogether I came home feeling suburban. Fearfully difficult, too, to talk simultaneously to the mission and laity, as represented by the Fox's and Mr. Edmunds. Mr. E. displays a healthy interest in walks and non-committal silence on religion. I don't think Mr. Fox approves of women who walk alone in the hills. When I told him of my nice lunch out of the wood-cutter's tummy-band, he looked very pensive.

We have a lovely spring day again, and I wish my foot would heal. It is nothing, but the place is awkward because it rubs against the shoe; and I suppose we can't count on much good weather this month. Mrs. F. told me they had to be dug out of the snow two years ago: and snow actually fell in Beirut and so frightened the population that all the *men* took to their beds.

Ever so much love to you both.

Your FREYA.

41. *To Miss Buddicom.*

BRUMANA. 7.2.28.

DEAREST VENETIA,

I have been trying in vain to send you a wire. India, they say, is not a sufficient address. It was to say that I have heard at last from Baghdad and that it is definitely off so far as I am concerned. Ja'far is being sent as representative to London. I am not really sorry, for there are many things to be done nearer. There will be time to plan when you come.

Meanwhile I hear you have to be inoculated for cholera

before reaching Syria from Iraq: otherwise they do it on
the border and may keep you five days outside Damascus.

Vaccination I suppose you have a certificate for? Beirut
full of smallpox just now. Brumana only measles so far.
And I found my first flea this morning—so that it really
looks like summer, doesn't it?

I have been hearing from people here about the ruined
cities of Bashan. That was what turned my thoughts to
Hauran. Delightful it is to have a little slice of World and
Time to play with. Do you know Marvell? But then he
says:

> "But at my back I always hear
> Time's winged chariot hurrying near,
> And yonder all before us lie
> Deserts of vast Eternity.

> "Let us roll all our strength and all
> Our sweetness up into one ball,
> And tear our pleasures with rough strife
> Through the iron gates of life."

Which seems sensible, doesn't it?
A rivederci, my dear. *Bon voyage*.

Your FREYA.

42. *To Clarmont P. Skrine.*

BRUMANA. 7.2.28.

MY DEAR CLARMONT,

I wonder if my letter to Birjand is still lying in some
Persian hiding-place? Or whether it followed you to
India? Or whether you were not really in India at all
when you sent me the picture? It has been giving me
pleasure ever since it came. I don't think I shall ever see
mountains enough to feel satisfied, and Nanga Parbat is
the right sort, with a proper solidity, not the fancy work of
the Dolomites that crumble into needles under the fingers
of the climber. Lebanon is good also. There is one
smooth snow ridge east of us, and a beautiful cone peak,

rather like Fujiyama, south, and we are on a ridge. Beirut lies flat as a map 2,800 feet below with twinkling evening lights, far more beautiful than she can ever be to anyone actually inside her.

It is so good to be out here at last, learning every day. I am getting at the Arabic through the tortuous ways of its own grammar, hoping that some day I may reach a country where the lovely classical is really used. Here they drop practically all the vowels, and have a tiresome habit of eliminating letters like q altogether. I had always suspected that one could live without minding p's and q's, but had never put it to the test!

The people are all charming to me. They are not really Eastern, nor anything: just a poor fringe of a people between Islam and the sea, doomed to be pawns in whatever politics are played here. All who can, emigrate to America, and all the money in the country comes from there. I haven't yet come across one spark of national feeling: it is all sects and hatreds and religions. I read the Maronite mass book the other day, and felt the prayer " to be saved from bloodshed " take on a particular meaning in this country of massacres. And it is a grand country, too.

Write when you have time: I shall be homesick for Asia!

Love from FREYA.

43. *To her Mother.*

BRUMANA. 8.2.28.

DEAREST B.,

Yesterday was Salehmy's birthday and he invited us all to a musical evening. Such a quaint gathering on the best chairs—raised velvet roses on a cream cotton background with green velvet edgings round the outlines. There was the charming old mother with a kind wrinkled peasant face and beautiful eyes still young: and four nondescript men in tarbooshes gradually individualized as Salehmy's brothers and nephews—masons, shoemakers, etc.: and a very pretty sister who teaches the convent orphans French: and a tiny niece who also possesses the family eyes, as yet only capable of expressing vast depths of curiosity. It was borne in upon me that I was the guest of the evening; my words were listened to in an interested silence which their strangeness deserves, but which I find trying. It appears that Salehmy had written all round to say that the music was for my special benefit; and I was much vexed when the doctor, who hasn't any idea of reticence in any form, took advantage of a moment's silence at the banquet to thank *me* as the cause of this delightful evening! I had an absurd feeling as if it were a betrothal, or I were so to speak assisting at my own funeral: Salehmy's mother taking farewell of me with three embraces, and her son and his sister presenting me with large bouquets of white roses in the midst of the silent but appreciative audience! The banquet was really very well done: a long, long table full of all sorts of wonderful things carried bodily into the passage outside the guest-room, and the family waited on us with charming dignified manners. They all know how to entertain here: no fuss, or effort.

We had lute, violin, and singing. At some of the wilder outbursts, M. Alexandre's eye was upon me with a *narquois* expression, saying as plainly as possible: "Were you really telling the truth when you said you *liked* this?" I am reserving judgment till I hear it out of doors with its own proper setting. As for the dancing, even Nijinski could hardly overcome the difficulties of a prosaic blue serge suit, shoes that haven't been polished for weeks, and stockings three sizes too large: but these details don't seem to worry the audience here in the least.

I have been reading Wells's latest. I think he has a second-rate mind—and how dangerous to invite Literary Lions to one's house. I should think the H's will hesitate another time.

Salehmy is making me read love poems, which I massacre. He sits and watches solemnly, except when the awful accents I give them rouse him to repressed frenzy. I can't pronounce the wretched "q", so that Love turns to "Thorns" in my version: I told him at last that was much the same meaning anyhow, and he now looks upon me as an authority on the ways of the heart!   I feel I am upsetting the village idea of the Average Englishwoman, so carefully built up by Quakers and Prayer, and am sorry, but what can I do.   I don't think anyone believes me when I tell them that I am interested only in the grammar.

Goodnight, dear B.

Your FREYA.

44. *To Mrs. Jeyes.*

BRUMANA.   10.2.28.

DARLING VIVA,

I hope my birthday greeting will not go to you from a bed of measles. The Spring has started like your infantile essay—cholera in Baghdad, smallpox in Damascus and Beirut, and measles here. The doctor, who is a dear, but irresponsible, invited us down the hill to walk with him. Miss Audi's weak heart disappears under excitement, and she came along in her high heels, and we motored by the mule track till the car really couldn't breast the obstacles. Then the doctor lost us in very pleasant terraces full of flowers and soft earth and finally we got to the village— just below us really—and found three sick children lying on their floor mattresses in the kitchen (very few here have beds). "Come in, come in," says the doctor, "and sit down," and only told us afterwards that it was measles.

The doctor's visits take a long time, because he sits and tells over all the family affairs, hears the children read their French, and is generally adored. Did you know that red curtains to your windows and red shades to your light are good for measles? That was the only part of the prescription I happened to be listening to. I was glad to get out into the sun again. The cottages, however, are cleaner than most Italian ones I have seen.

We are all supposed to be re-vaccinated and not allowed in Beirut without fresh certificates. Unfortunately, the doctor has lost the vaccine. His cousin told me in private this afternoon. Brumana still thinks the precious stuff is on its way from Palestine and would be annoyed to know that it is probably poisoning a ditch by the highway.

The doctor's cousin, Miss Bennington, has just come out from England and is very restive under what she calls "their slipshod ways". My Italian training comes in useful: I find myself quite placid under trial. The advantages of a Continental education! I have managed only one bath since I came, and have to wash in cold water every evening, and my room has nothing but pegs and a table—and it is all quite bearable. But Miss B. thinks it heroic.

Venetia wires she is not coming till 15th April, so I shall stay in Damascus first. Better address to the Consulate. I hear that Consul and Missionaries are all the British there, and the French are loathed, so I should get enough Arabic to speak.

The world is all almond blossom and anemones,

Your own FREYA.

45. *To Miss Buddicom.*

BRUMANA.   11.2.28.

DEAREST VENETIA,

Providence, or whatever inspired your telegram, does seem to be doing things for the best. April will be far better than March, and you will have heard by now that I am free as air. If you can be induced not to reach home till June, who knows but what we may pull off Rum after all.

I go about 10th March to Damascus and will wait for you there or thereabouts. It seems a bad moment. The Christians and Moslems at loggerheads over a Danish pastor. But whether it is *all* Christians, or only the missionaries, I can't tell till I get there.

I seem unable to get a Mohammedan lodging as I had hoped. All these things take time and time, and oh! how I wish I had a whole language, or even a good half, instead of the little bit of it I have to make grow. It really is the secret of travelling. The dullest country has a soul of some sort if you can know what its people are saying—not only the words but the thoughts that make them.

You will be amused. It appears that the theory here is that I am a spy for the British. I am entertained, and only hope that the same bright thought won't enter the French heads too and bother us while travelling. We shall be all right this side of Damascus, but probably find difficulties if we want to go south at all.

Do remember the wash basin.

At present one can pick up measles in any cottage, but that I hope will be over.

My news is no news except grammar. I haven't read a book to call a book since I came, except Wells's romance of Mortola. I do think it is rather too bad to depict your hostess as a murderess and dedicate the book to her!

Don't come a day later than April 15 or it will be too hot. The climate seems as unsafe as the Syrian dog: he comes wagging his tail and, when you pat him, bites your hand off. Mine was saved by my coat sleeve.

Good it will be to see you.

Your FREYA.

46. *To her Mother*.

BRUMANA. 12.2.28.

DEAREST B.,

We picnicked at Deir el Qal'a yesterday, an old temple to Jupiter of the Dancing Floor and some Phoenician god before him. It is high up on a spur, and the Phoenician blocks now enclose a small garden belonging to the Maronite monks. The almond flowers hang out over the old smooth stone, and there is a good snowy amphitheatre of hills standing well away across the valley. We saw a white tip, and Salehmy said Hermon, but people are Liars about topography.

It was a very ill-assorted party: Miss Bennington normal British; Mlle. disposed to flirt with M. Alexandre who was placid but bored; and Salehmy whose French is so peculiar. I found walking between him and Miss B. trying, acting as *trait-d'union* between what refuses to amalgamate. Mr. A. made a determined effort to walk back with us, but Mlle. has all the obstinacy of the People of Feeling, and collared

him. I should have liked less social talk, and time to
wander among the old columns and lovely yellow stone.
It is a great building country; the stone seems easy to
work and hard; the colour of it simply delicious. We
came back by the rough road, made out of sight of the
coast by Turks for their guns; a gun and some old trenches
are still there below the monastery, derelict.

Your own FREYA.

47. *To Lady Waller.*

BRUMANA.   12.2.28.

DEAREST DOT,

I wonder if you are going out to inhabit poor
neglected l'Arma, which is longing for someone to enjoy
its flowers? This should arrive for your birthday and
bring you loving greetings.

I get no time except for writing home. Four or five
hours study a day, and the rest all talking! Now and then
I get a good day with "sandwiches and the beauties of
nature". I spend my time resisting kindness and advice.
All here are charming, and anxious to prevent my being
killed by some irritated Druse, but I feel if once I begin
to do what I am told I shall very soon be carrying the
donkey. Do you remember how we used to gallop our
ponies to the very last minute and always have to creep
in the back way not to be discovered? That is how I
intend to treat my tiresome little body; the animal creature
should be animated, says I, and not go its own lazy way.

This Christian country is divided into fierce and venomous little sects. The Druses are dignified and keep
whatever their religion may be very properly to themselves,
ready to massacre the Others if the opportunity should
come, but otherwise polite.

What I find trying in a country which you do not understand and where you cannot speak, is that you can never
be *yourself.* You are English, or Christian, or Protestant,
or anything but your individual *you*: and whatever you say
or do is fitted to the label and burdened with whatever
misdeeds (or good deeds) your predecessors may have

F

committed. And then of course your sentences, intended
with just the shade of meaning you desire, come out shorn
of all accessories, quite useless for anything except the
mere procuring of bread and butter. How glad I shall
be when I can feel that the country is really *mine*, not
the mere panorama to the stranger. Meanwhile the world
is open. I feel that my seven years' patience is rewarded
with Rebecca straightaway, and am very happy.

Viva will have told you about the country. Its glorious
great hills and snowy spaces. And the almond trees in
blossom now. The people pleasant to meet; no future,
and no grit out of which such things are made, but very
agreeable and many of them beautiful. One might say
as much Italian again as Italy.

Send me news of Thornworthy and all there.

Your loving FREYA.

48. *To Herbert Young.*

BRUMANA. 16.2.28.

MY DEAR HERBERT,

Where are you? Rome, Mortola, London? It is
hard to write when one can't imagine where one is talking
to, and I suppose you will have heard my news wherever
you may be.

I am thriving on Curds and Christianity, or what goes
for such (for this is a terribly good place). The Mission
is, I believe, slowly recovering from its first delusion as
to my being among the sheep, but they are all very kind
and full of help and advice for Damascus next month.
But, sad to relate, all the Syrians seem secretly relieved
to have someone non-missionary among them: I think they
are overdone with these competitive religions. I have
come to the conclusion that the only way to be a missionary
is just to be a Christian and say no more about it; to do it
this way by committees seems to me a *horrible* interference
with rightful liberties.

I think of beloved l'Arma wasting its flowers. I wonder
if you are there, and how things are?

I am a little tired of being a mystery. To learn Arabic

for pleasure is simply not done, and as I have no other reason to give, I get credit for marvellous secrecy: also for being either a novelist or a spy! I told my landlady about Ibn Saud's 173 wives, and this piece of true history has impressed her deeply with my knowledge of politics. It is all such fun.

Loving wishes to all,

Yours affectionately, FREYA.

49. *To her Mother.*

BRUMANA. 16.2.28.

DARLING B.,

I think I shall number my letters, for I hear that many are lost in the censorship. I heard all sorts of tales from Mrs. Cruikshank yesterday. The doctor took me down to Beirut. I was firm with him and refused to go round and visit his patients and was rewarded by a comfortable tea surrounded by old Damascus silver, and a pleasant hostess who wants me to spend a week-end later. The only trouble was that the hours were passing, suppertime coming on (theirs, mine had long gone by) and no one ever knows when the doctor will come back. I got up to go, but there *is* nowhere to go to in the wilds of Beirut. However, he came just in time, and after leaving me another half-hour on a starlit doorstep where I was able to watch six Syrians trying to pack themselves and one coffin into a taxi, we finally climbed up into a deluge from that pleasant warm climate down below.

The store of wood has given out here, so we have nothing but the brazier: and Mlle. so distressed I have to comfort her and pretend that I sit in my fur coat out of mere caprice.

She will be pleased with your note to her. The Manassehs' I won't give, because you talk about their giving me *advice*, which is the one thing I am trying to discourage. I like to be helped, with as little advice as possible, for that seems to be exclusively composed of Better Nots.

The Manassehs are extremely kind. She is pretty and

dresses nicely, rather absent-minded, fond of sketching, and placid enough to have survived in a gentle dreamy way through the unpunctual chaos of the doctor's life.

Tell George the boxes arrived beautifully, and no duty to pay. Thank him so much in the name of my complexion.

I am beginning to feel a little tired: my third month without a day off except Sundays and Xmas Day, and it is a strain to listen to a strange language. I find myself slipping into inertia and letting the words go by in an unintelligible stream. Salehmy also is getting inattentive, letting me go unchecked my ungrammatical way. He and Mlle. and M. Alexandre want to come and see me in Damascus. I do enjoy seeing Mlle. flirt a little; it is so good for her, and a natural form of exercise after all.

I shall try and write to Herbert next.

Your own FREYA.

50. *To her Mother.*

BRUMANA. 19.2.28.

DEAREST B.,

I have just been to mass at the Greek Church, with four beautiful gold ikons to look at. I liked the service, what I could understand of it. The priest's scarlet cope and long black hair and beard look very effective as he comes in and out from behind the screen where the Communion is celebrated. The singing is very clever: they replace the organ by a sustained humming—louder than humming but yet not singing, varying between four and five notes and forming a sort of background to the voices of the chanters. The people are pleased if one goes to their service. I have now been to Maronite, Orthodox and Greek Catholic: on the whole I think I liked this Greek Orthodox best. I was amused to see in the Maronite mass that they pray for "our fathers, brothers and teachers," a complete exclusion of our sex, you observe. To-day they were having a service for the dead, which we did not stay for, but I thought of Macugnaga, for there was a dish of sweets on a table in front of the altar screen and they were to be distributed in memory of the dead man. It

must be a very old custom to have travelled so far as Monte
Ross̄

The priest from Aleppo and his sister came to spend
the evening.   You will be amused to hear that I was called
upon to sing, and did so too with great success!   Mlle's
refined little soul does not take to the priest and his sister,
who are the Don Odoberto type, a little broad I imagine.
I find it comforts her greatly to hear that the "hill" priests,
which here is contrary to "town," are just as bad in Italy.

Religion is a delicate point.   Now that she realizes I
don't want to turn people into Presbyterians, or anything
else for that matter, it is all coming out: all the bottled-
up feelings since the time when her brother turned Quaker
and she came into contact with all the People who Think
They Know Better: and never said anything, but just (I
believe) hated them more and more.   These people never
contradict: they listen politely while the convinced missionary goes blundering on—annoyed afterwards that they
"turn round".   But I believe the fact is that they don't
"turn round".   They have simply *never turned at all*:
only their politeness is never to say *No* when an Englishman
would say so: in fact to say *Yes*.

Must stop now.

Your loving FREYA.

51.   *To Herbert Young.*

BRUMANA.   19.2.28.

MY DEAR HERBERT,

What a lovely time you will be having in the garden
now—everything just beginning.   Here also one feels
the spring, though when the north wind blows it is like
a blast of sheer ice.

I regret more than ever that I was not properly and
thoroughly brought up on the Bible.   Who were the
Amalekites and Hittites?   And what happened in Bashan?
The Hittites, I discover, lived north of us with their capital
near Aleppo at a place called Kadesh, and they used to
wear red shoes: the same as one still buys in Antioch no
doubt.   It is all good country if one were not so ignorant.

A feeling of intense age about it—rather hopeless too. My beautiful snow ridge, Sannin, was once Her not the Palestine one but a brother; and Byblos of the Giblites, who I believe used to make boats, is along the coast. This actual country belonged to the Amalekites: and that is as much Useful Information as I can give you to-day, except that I suppose the frequent blue eyes one meets must have been due to regrettable incidents during the crusades. There are a great many of them.

I am glad you have the joy of a new Rolls. It is hard to be poor: I am always feeling it. All one has must go in luxuries, and the necessities must just be done without!

Dear Herbert, how lovely to get back and sit in *warm* Asolo, beside the little Bacchus.

Ever your FREYA.

52. *To her Mother.*

BRUMANA.   22.2.28.

DARLING B.,

It is the most infamous weather you can imagine, and unfortunate that the wood supply has given out. I sit in my furs, with every reserve of natural stoicism, and console myself by thinking of the Psalms, which seem peculiarly suited to this country: the same abrupt transitions, and everything done on a big scale: and the malignant suddenness with which storms sweep down out of a blue sky to overwhelm, is very like Jehovah at his worst. I am waiting for their pleasanter aspect in the Spring, and to hear the voice of the turtle dove: at present it is only the little yelping jackals, who go running about the valleys with a great noise as soon as the stars come out. When they bark much, it means clear frosty weather.

Poor Mrs. Manasseh is nearly exhausted because two men came to her on Saturday and said that one of them was going to marry her cook next day. A pretty girl, and she had no particular wish to marry the man, who squints. Argument was vain, however, and as it was the last day before Lent and no marrying for two months, there was nothing for it: they spent a hectic day sewing the essential

underwear: the bridegroom sent a white frock and old
silver shoes: there were streams of relatives all day drinking
coffee and eating cakes: and finally Mrs. Manasseh took
the bride and bride's mother to the church at 8 p.m. on a
gusty evening. The priest seemed to have forgotten all
about it, and couldn't be found till someone had the bright
idea of tolling the church bell for him. Luckily everyone
carried a candle, so the ceremony was not performed in
pitch darkness. Mrs. Manasseh returned exhausted to her
cookless home, and is now being assisted by the bride's family,
who are full of gratitude, and only ignorant of cookery.

I have a letter from Mrs. Robertson, full of love and
intelligence. She is a wonderful and dear person.

Mr. Chamoun came to examine my Arabic, and was
quite pleased. He says he has noticed I say I know less
than I really do: which Miss Audi corroborates with
adjectives. I don't think this is true, but I suppose I try
not to assume I know *more*, and it shows the value of
understatement in principle. Agostino once told me that
British diplomacy, when it merely speaks the truth, which
happens quite frequently, is therefore credited with all
the things *it doesn't say*!

I shall be glad of a holiday. My first three months
steady work after convalescing are about as much as I
can manage, and I shall take it easy in Damascus.

Salehmy has written a poem about our picnic. He
compares us to "chaste gazelles". I forget the other
adjectives, but if only you could see Miss B. and Mrs.
Manasseh meandering over rocks; anything less like a
gazelle! It is very funny. I wonder if I can resist the
temptation of telling them.

Your own FREYA.

53. *To her Father*.

BRUMANA. 23.2.28.

DARLING PIPS,

I hope you are a great deal warmer than I am.

We had an earthquake last night; quite slight, but
enough to give a gyrating sensation to one's legs. It had

been pouring all day (it still is) and we were sitting after supper, Mlle., my teacher Salehmy and I, over our little green table by the fire when a noise came rushing along— an inorganic sort of roar. I wish I had been paying more attention. I was not thinking, and only knew what it was from Mlle's paralysed expression, and when I tried to get up found it quite difficult to move—for less than a second— because of the wobbliness of the room. I have often wondered whether I should be one of the people who say "*Après vous*" in fires and shipwrecks. The truth is, I was half-way to the door to see if it would open, and then remembered Mlle's chronic need of moral support and nobly waited to hold her hand into the passage. By this time everything was long over, and we devoted ourselves to eau de Cologne and ether for her fluttering nerves. I was so pleased to feel what sort of a movement it is. Only hope it does not mean any destruction somewhere round about.

This is a disgusting climate in February. The wind is like ice, and handfuls of hail, thunder, lightning and rain are flung at us in the intervals. If we were not on a high hill and the soil all sand we should have been drowned long ago. When it is given a chance, the view is marvellous. The north wind turns the sea blue and green and the sun-sets fill it with delicate pastel reflections, and light up the hills and snow as if the door of a blazing furnace were opened on to them. The rock itself here has a great variety of colours. I found bright red stone, grey, black, yellow, pink. All lime I imagine, from the number of old kilns everywhere. There are millions of buried fossils, just like Mortola, so that one thinks of the Mediterranean more than ever as the pond where the world's infants first started playing pirates.

Your own FREYA.

54. *To her Mother.*

BRUMANA. 26.2.28.

DARLING B.,

First glimpses of sun to-day for a week. Rain, snow, thunder, all the time, and my room 5 centigrade,

and the sitting-room 7.   As we have so little wood we can
only have a fire in the evening   The day before yesterday
I threw up the sponge and went to bed to keep warm and
spent *such* a happy day, and half the next day too.

Oh blessed sun.   I am going out now at last.

Your FREYA.

55.   *To her Mother.*

BRUMANA.   26.2.28.

DARLING B.,

The last days of carnival were celebrated by one
really satisfactory elopement to balance the sad wedding of
the Manassehs' cook.   It seems there was a very pretty
young girl in the village, and she was loved by her poor
young cousin and by a rich elderly man in Beit Meri.
The father decided on the latter, and the thing was settled
with the usual haste, and she was told to get ready to be
married.   But the young men of the village heard of it,
and five or six of them came to the door while her father
had gone for the bridegroom, and just as she had got
through her bath and was only half dressed.   They banged
on the door, and asked her which she wanted, the young
or the old one.   "The young one," says she very properly.
"Then open the door."   One of the youths hoisted her on
his back and threw his coat over her: another followed
with the slippers and a bundle of clothes: another went to
find the bridegroom (who did not even know that the elderly
marriage had been settled at all).   They found a priest and
a motor car, and went off and got the marriage over before
the parents came home.   Salehmy told us all this last
night, and seemed much surprised that I should approve
of youth and poverty.

I was going to meeting this morning, but met Miss B.
and went for a walk instead, to enjoy the first sun and
listen to her woes.   It seems the doctor left her with his wife
ill on her hands, and no wood in the house, and sent all
the servants off for the afternoon, so that she had a stream
of Arabic-speaking people to deal with at the door, and
when he came back he found her in a state of acute exasperation, clamouring for wood and servants.   He merely

said in his gentle way: "You are upset," took down a little
book, and began reading out a long prayer. She gathered
herself together and listened without a murmur, said
thank you, and: "May I now have my wood, please?"
But she came out in quite a venomous frame of mind!

I have written . . . a peaceful sort of letter. Hope it
does not have the same effect as the doctor's prayer.

27.2.28.

I nearly wept this morning when I woke to another
fiendish day. Breakfast in bed has no charm when one has
to wrap one's handkerchief round the knife handle so as not
to be frozen. The good old man who lives an hour's
walk down the valley and brings the wood up on his ancient
back knew of our troubles, and came pattering up in inadequate slippers under a load, wet to the bone: I have now
brought the room to comparative comfort at 10 centigrade
and succeeded in persuading Mlle. to keep the door shut,
and we do not stir from the house. It is just like Mortola
rain, only this is its third week. Twenty-eight inches in
three months is not bad for the sunny south.

Yesterday was an interval, a lovely evening and starry
night. I dined as usual on Sunday with the Fox's. It is a
lovely walk in the moonlight: the ridge here so aloof that it
seems you are looking down on the lower stars. The new
moon very clear and frosty was throwing a bar of light
behind Beirut, twinkling like a cluster of topazes down
below, and the two lights made a wonderful contrast
together. The moon seemed peculiar: not turned either
east or west but lying flat on her back, and if Herbert can
explain this Syrian idiosyncracy (and please remember it
was a teetotal missionary dinner with only cocoa after) I
shall be very glad.

I believe I am more approved of now that I go to Sunday
meetings. Mr. Edmunds, who is a delightful young man
with the merit of a nice profile and just about as incongruous here as I am, approves of me anyway. This is so
satisfactory because I am suffering from the pinched
expression peculiar to old age or a cold climate, and looking
in the mirror I came to the conclusion that it *must* be my
soul, since nothing else worth approving of is visible. And

how nice to have the sort of soul that is liked by people with agreeable profiles!

I had just written to Mrs. More when I read that the Wahabis are marching on Kuweit and a British boat sent to look after them: so they will be having a busy time.

Poor Salehmy is getting so thin with the cold. He comes shivering every night. I offered him my waterproof to go down to the school to-night, but he assures me that all that matters is his tarboosh and he has gone through the deluge under a small umbrella. I have never known people who mind physical discomforts so little. I suppose when you are accustomed to being massacred, you don't trouble about the minor things. Even if it is pouring with rain, Mlle. always has to remind Marie the maid to take her umbrella. She said to me to-day: "How do you manage in England through the long winter? I suppose you keep warm by always walking?" Visions of Napier, bedroom fires and curtains and carpets! I gave up even the effort to describe.

Ever your own FREYA.

56. *To her Mother.*

BRUMANA. 1.3.28.

DARLING B.,

I felt in my bones your letter was coming to-day, and here it is—such a good long one.

The clothes sound lovely, and you tell me they will *wash.* That is indispensable, in case I go in third-class carriages or among the Beduin poor. As for the silk, I can't imagine ever wanting anything cool to wear any more.

We are still alive, though wizened. Miss Audi thanked me to-day for suggesting the shutting of the sitting-room door, which has been open through all these winters till I came!

On Sunday nights I get a good warm up at Mrs. Fox's fire before the meeting, and a hot cup of cocoa after: and then Mr. F. and Mr. Edmunds see me home. Who could refuse to pray when so sandwiched? As a matter of fact, I like Mr. Fox particularly and the Quaker hymn tunes are mostly good. It is only the inappropriateness to this civilization that I object to.

Mr Edmunds lectured on Russia yesterday. He spent a year and a half there doing relief work, and it was pleasant for a change to listen to someone whose thoughts are well arranged with a thread running through them, and who has something to say and is not merely filling up thirty minutes with words. He has a taste for ideas, which is pleasant. I do like people who have not yet made up their minds about everything, who in fact are still *receiving*: taking up new impressions, and assimilating them, and adding bits to the philosophy one builds up for one's old age. That is youth really: not a matter of years. And to remember that other people are coming along too, building in new and different fashions; and to remain pleased with it all and keen, like dear Mrs. Robertson who never grows old.

Mrs. Fox, by the way, must be a bit negligent or how could she let the young man go about with pockets that need darning so badly.

Your own FREYA.

57. *To her Father.*

BRUMANA. 1.3.28.

DARLING PIPS,

We thought, we really did think, that we should wake up to a fine day this morning. When Marie told me it was snowing I thought it a joke. It was the Padre Eterno's joke, however, and we are still at it; everyone looking a little pale and worn. It would be all right if there were anywhere to get warm at all, but the sitting-room here, with fire and brazier, is only 8 centigrade: to-morrow our small wood supply is going to give out. All the goats are being hurried down from the higher villages. They are nice animals, mostly black, with curly horns and long droopy hair with a silky wave to it. There was one little kid skipping about in a world too cold for it, and they looked very fine coming down over the white hillside with goatherds tramping behind in their red woollen swathings and headcloths tied round their caps for warmth.

Even the gramophone has caught cold. It is Mlle's newest treasure, and we had an anxious time over the noises it was making. But yesterday several experts came to call, and we held it over the brazier and allowed it to go round and round till it gradually recovered. Several cheerful young Syrians came and made a lemon ice which they all seemed to enjoy. I prefer dancing; anything to get warm. A knock at the door in the middle of it sent us all scuffling back to our places, for we thought it was the doctor, who would have been surprised and pained to see the headmaster pirouetting so gaily.

The earthquake last week came in the midst of Mr. Edmunds' lecture: so suitable, as he was talking of Bolsheviks: but they did not feel it much on the ground floor. It did a little damage in Palestine.

Last night the poor hyena which lives in the valley apparently made its way into the street outside the butcher's shop. Salehmy put his head out of window and saw it surrounded by angry dogs, but when he got back with his revolver it had vanished. That is what he tells us.

The French have just published a decree condemning a lot of Druse chiefs to death, or rather confirming their previous condemnation. They are all safe across the border, but it must be annoying, and I wish they had waited till V. and I are through our little tour. There is general animation. Wahibis in Iraq, and tribal affairs across Jordan. I begin to read the local papers and get much fun out of them. I spent a long time yesterday trying to make out two words in Arabic which turned out to be Sir Alfred Mond's name. The Baghdad students greeted him with such anti-Zionist demonstrations that 150 of them have been "sent down".

I have not heard of my room in Damascus. The Pass is probably blocked, and no news coming through. The post to the higher villages here had to go on mule-back instead of by car to-day, and the ridge between us and Damascus is much higher. But the snow here will melt with two days' sun.

So much love, dearest Pips.   Your FREYA.

58. *To her Mother.*

BRUMANA. 3.3.28.

DARLING B.,

We had an afternoon at the Chamouns' yesterday to eat "Tabouli," a delicious salad made of ground corn, mint and parsley. You eat it out of a big dish in the middle of the table, using lettuce leaves and fingers to scoop it up with. I was offered a fork, but of course refused. I do feel a little sadder for it to-day; alas that experience will be paid for!

It is still extremely cold, but sunny. Five of the school-boys down with pneumonia, and everyone looking slightly the worse: people creep out like beetles from their holes to whatever patch of sun is nearest.

We are going to Jubeil to-morrow. I wanted to take the Chamouns somewhere, and Miss B. and Mr. Edmunds have got added on and will no doubt amuse each other. Jubeil was Byblos—Gebal of the Phoenicians, along the coast northwards.

Yesterday I went to the Municipio to help in the vaccination of the village. As it turned out, there was no help needed except the occasional buttoning up of some small infant; but it was very amusing to watch the various types —so very various, blue eyes and black, from the rather loosely put together northern features to clear portraits from the old Assyrian: occasionally a streak of negro; occasionally good aquiline. I hope to see more of that in Damascus. There was much chaff; the doctor going on unmoved, scratching with his little knife his 200th leg or arm that day and disinfecting over a spirit lamp between each scratch. The local soldiery (who are really made use of in a great variety of ways) wrote out the certificates. Great giggles among the ladies, who do not like to exhibit their legs to a roomful of men: and I must say it was very public. An occasional outburst of wails from the infants, who usually, however, rolled up quite independently and very solemn, and managed the whole affair by themselves, holding up their little sleeves with great gravity. The method of strengthening people by starvation and murder seems absurd, but there is no doubt it appears to work here. They are as hardy as can be. When you think of them as compared to Italy, it is like thinking of iron and earthenware: you feel these people are hard *all through*. I imagine that what is wrong with them is just what was wrong with their Phoenician ancestors: they have no imagination; therefore no ideals, or not sufficient to make them really do something. I am reading about Phoenicia, and it seems that all their genius went into practical things and manual execution. And so, in a degenerated way, it still goes on, and the Syrians spread over the world, America, Australia, no matter how far, making money and thinking about money.

People are kind, and say they are sorry I am going. I am sorry too, and feel as if tearing up roots. What a dreadful disposition it is to get fond of people wherever one goes.

Always your loving FREYA.

59. *To her Father.*

BRUMANA. 5.3.28.

DEAREST PIPS,

I cannot get to Damascus because there is still too much snow. The train goes, but it takes ten hours and no heating, and I have no news of my room. I have just been reading in the Arabic paper that if you get your ticket in two parts, interrupting the journey that is to say, you pay twice as much for it. An unlucky traveller did this, expecting to be met half-way by a car: when he reached the junction, and found nothing but snow, he got into his train again and continued with a new ticket: and discovered this peculiar arrangement. I am only mentioning it because of Salehmy's and Mlle's conclusions on the matter. Salehmy believes that the railway company takes advantage of the absence of cars to make an extra profit. Mlle. says that one's ticket would naturally be more expensive in bad weather. This, I imagine, is the Syrian's idea of law. Anyway, I have made up my mind to travel on a fine day.

It was a good day for Byblos yesterday. It is a small
enough place now, on a low half circle of land between
the hills and the sea, sloping gently. There was one sleepy
bazaar street: one looks up at it through an arch, and they
have had the happy thought to paint all their shutters a
gentle turquoise blue, which gives to the whole street the
dreaminess of water. There was a little portico close to
the church, faded to delicious ochre and with a different
moulding to each of its three arches; crusading work, I
thought, for one of the rolled mouldings was certainly
Norman. I wish I knew more about these things. Miss B.,
however, informed us without knowing, which is quite
entertaining if not taken seriously. I don't know enough
to enjoy the bare bones of archaeology when there is no
beauty to clothe them. The Phoenician graveyard looked
so much like a rubbish heap. The huge sarcophagi are
cut out of single blocks of stone, with monolithic lids and
knobs sticking out of them (for the ropes I suppose), and
they used to be lowered into the underground chambers
on mounds of sand which was carried away in sackloads
from under them so that their level gradually sank. They
are impressive by sheer weight, but it is a cast-iron art
after all and makes one feel what an unpleasant people
the Phoenicians must have been. The remains of their
gods (or goddesses here) are just as repulsive, though there
was a forlornness about them, the desolation of the passing
of Time. There are four great trunks, broken off at the
thighs, and roughly hewn in stone, standing facing the
sea and the west with a stupid and pathetic obstinacy of a
dead religion passed beyond all change. The outlines of
the temple are still there among debris and weeds, eloquent
to the eyes of the expert.

The castle was much more human and cheerful, with a
bridge and a moat (dry), guard room, banqueting hall,
and secret passage to the sea—all the objects one expects
in a castle: and narrow steps to climb, and a grass-grown
roof for Sister Anne to walk on. Mr. Edmunds found his
way to my heart by clambering about with the pure joy
that every normal human being ought to take in battlements. Miss B. lingered, fabricating theories of most
surprising incorrectness. The other two poor ladies had

long ago sunk exhausted on a Phoenician block and were, I suspect, talking about food, for the lunch hour had long gone by.

We wanted to lunch in the Banqueting Hall, where an ancient stone table was all ready propped on stone pillars: but the Syrian ladies had set their hearts on Adonis stream farther back along the coast. They found us a place with little tin tables near the river, in what they considered rural surroundings, just below the iron bridge and all among the empty bottles. Miss B. and Mr. Edmunds were frankly rebellious; Mr. Chamoun and I held an intermediate position, trying to reconcile national prejudices. We felt it was the ladies' turn, after their forlorn morning; and they were allowed to pull out forks and spoons and cups and arrange the most suburban meal, and murmur (in Arabic luckily) how lovely the view was—till after lunch, and then we left them again and turned our backs on the road and all its horrors, and soon found Adonis flowing among clefts, clear green, a strong and lovely stream. It was very like good hill country. We wandered up the valley in warm sunlight, the river winding round corners, far down.

We looked perpendicularly on it, and across at zigzag paths the other side, and houses and a tree or two against the skyline, incredibly steep. It is a barren country. Down below, just where an eighteenth century landscape painter would have put it, was a great ruin of an arch: Zenobia's, said Miss B., making the poor lady wander. We were really quite contented. I was at any rate. And Mr. Edmunds told us it was his first day of peace since his arrival last September, a terrible light on moral wear and tear among the Quakers. I found three red anemones: then we eked them out with the deep crimson poppies that stand in the grass along the lower reaches of the stream and climbed up on to the Roman bridge, which is the shape of a rainbow. We flung the flowers down and watched them float away like rubies in the sun on the green water, a lovely sight, and the first offering Adonis has had for a long time I expect. And it was pleasant to see the Syrian Headmaster of a Missionary School sacrificing to his ancestral gods.

Before we got home the moon was hanging over us:

G

very near it seemed, she rises so suddenly over these steep round hills. The road goes up through a deep-cut quarry, and we came out of blackness into the gentle light, the shining sea below. Beautiful world. Eternity does put on lovely garments. We were fifteen minutes late, and Mrs. Fox so painfully polite over it.

                                    Your loving FREYA.

60.   *To Mrs. Jeyes.*

                                    BRUMANA.   8.3.28.

DEAREST VIVA,

        What an inspiration to send me Gertrude Bell. It is *wonderful*; a breath of the world and its spaces. And I hope it will also be of great use. It has certainly given me more information than I can get here, for everyone is incredibly vague.

Your letter came this morning, with the piece of ribbon most suitable to carry in my pocket and give away in bits in return for food and coffee. The others you mention were evidently too fascinating for the P.O., and I have not received them.

At last I have a Druse guide for April. The doctor was so obstinate about it, assuring me that a Christian was better. I felt convinced this was not so. And now the Christian has settled the matter by refusing to go into the Druse country, saying he would be killed. I am so much relieved. Now we have a man and mule and donkey, all for 10s. a day, and an itinerary marked out by the doctor. Imshallah, may it come about.

I have got my room in Damascus. It doesn't sound too attractive, for the missionary lady says that my hostess "is a dear but grasping," and would I like my meals in my bedroom "as the men's table manners are so bad?" I shall try and put up with the manners for the sake of the accent.

I saw a good castle on Sunday: old yellow walls laid on great blocks without mortar—Phoenician foundations. The Crusaders built up from them, jamming slices of pagan columns into their main walls. These round grey objects jutting out untidily from the yellow stone of the rest have a diseased look: quite suitable to the aimless tangle of the history of this land.

Your loving FREYA.

61. *To her Mother.*

BRUMANA. 8.3.28.

DARLING B.,

You will get all the news from the enclosed, so I can devote myself to the ecstasy of clothes. They really are adorable. Thank you ever so. What I have been longing for is little flounces.

Mr. Napier's suggestion will not do. The one thing Consuls here are anxious to discourage is ladies travelling about and giving trouble. They do not like people to die out of their beds, and are always worrying about that.

My lessons have come to an end. I have given Salehmy an Italian present, I hope it will please him. He has given me *all* my lesson books, and has now brought me an Arabic *Life of St. Theresa,* and the letter to the Druse prince.

Your own FREYA.

62. *To her Mother.*

BRUMANA. 9.3.28.

DARLING B.,

I will add a line as I forgot to post my letter yesterday, though there is no news except that Venetia now wires to suggest *May.* I have telegraphed to implore her to stick to April, for I must manage a fortnight's rest between the Druses and the journey home.

The snow is hardly melting on the hills, and there are rumours that the Damascus road is still impassable. The train goes through, however.

A lot of exiles from the Druse revolt have just come home with wild welcomings in Damascus. The French are a good deal more liberal than the Italians in their censorship: the newspaper went into rhapsodies over these people "who had sacrificed all for the freedom of their country, and whose sacrifice will surely not be vain", So it said. Imagine anyone talking like that in an Italian paper.

I seem to have caused an awful splash in the mission pond by carrying people off from their Sunday prayers. Possibly there will be another splash to-night, for Mr. Edmunds is coming to supper. Miss Audi's heart is already melting at the thought of Romance, which she transmutes very laudably into the menu. "Monsieur Edmond is very intelligent. Do you think he will like caramel pudding?" seems to be the gist of her conversation all to-day. I am getting our food and his virtues completely mixed.

I called yesterday to say good-bye to Salehmy's mother and found a banquet prepared, a table heaped with good things. I find that the only way out is to seize on whatever is portable, and say you "will take it with you".

I have so many calls to pay. Four yesterday, and ended at the teacher's tea table at school. I had M. Alexandre on one side, Salehmy on the other, Mr. Edmunds opposite, and was thinking over the differences of the three races. In the middle of my meditations I found Mr. Chamoun's eye fixed on me with an expression of such intense amusement, I would give something to know exactly what was passing through his mind. Perhaps he was thinking of Sunday.

To-morrow some people from the Central Friends' Committee will be here and we are all asked to tea and to see football after. Shall I wear my nicest frills? I do feel I have been good for so long. Luckily Mrs. Fox so approves of my respectable introductions that she swallows me as well. She only made the gentlest remark about Sundays in general, and has been really so kind: and I feel I must have been a trial, landing here from the blue without knowing a soul: and everything I do, the most ordinary things that everybody does in any sensible place, gives them electric shocks all round.

Next letter from Damascus, I hope.

Your own FREYA.

63. *To her Mother.*

BRUMANA. 11.3.28.

DARLING B.,

This is my last letter from Brumana till May, and I am feeling so depressed, like a waif starting off into the unknown again, now that I have been settled here so long. Everything seems to have swelled itself out too, like a pony when you saddle it, so that I can't be contained in my boxes.

The guide however is found, and his name is Najm—star —surely a good omen. He is middle-aged, sturdy, with lively brown eyes, a moustache with a twist to it, and a red sash round his middle: and he promises to see to us, body and soul, till we are safe through the Druse country: and will show us all the old castles and the modern ruins by the way. May it go smoothly!

I had a pleasant day yesterday with charming Mr. Edmunds, who turned his back in a lovely blue coat with brass buttons on all the Sunday ceremonies and came wandering. He is good at the walking, only he had never been off a road before, and discovered with surprise that Lebanon paths are stony. Somehow we got enticed off the path, too, and descended over ledges down to the river, sliding down rocks of a torrent bed along the path of the waterfalls; it was very creditable, for he didn't just set his teeth and bear it, but I believe quite enjoyed it and talked of mountaineering in Italy. I enjoyed talking like a human being again after nearly four months' starvation; I suddenly realized how long it had been! We had egg sandwiches beside the stream—rushing green water now, and no skipping over stepping stones like last time.

We found a real tree, not merely a pine, and sat in shade, and watched an eagle turning its great flat head slowly in the sun and, after a long time, flapping across the valley over our heads. The river is a long way down: we were made excessively aware of it by having to rush up the hill at speed so that he might be back by five—and we did it with one minute to spare, but my heart was pounding like a hammer all night: I must be getting old. The old wood-cutter who came through the rain was ill: we passed his cottage and stopped for a drink of water and found him lying on a mattress beside his earthenware stove, but quite cheerful. Nice old man. Two goatherds, also, we talked to; they looked so well in their old red jackets and muffled up heads among the black browsing goats and speckled shadows. One of them came up with the first black kidling in the crook of his arm, born that day, a little leggy anatomy, soft as silk.

I must finish off the packing.

Your own FREYA.

Telling of a month at Damascus, where the writer stayed in a native household in the Moslem quarter, and was much hampered by ill-health due to insanitary conditions. After three weeks' convalescence in Brumana she is joined by her friend Venetia Buddicom, whose acquaintance the reader has already made in the course of this correspondence.

64. *To her Father.*

TRAIN TO DAMASCUS. 14.3.28.

DEAREST PIPS,

The snow is still heavy on the Pass and we are crawling towards it at an incredibly slow pace: it takes nine and a half hours for less than a hundred miles. I have a Syrian family with me: we spend the time eating: last station they dashed out for "leban," the milky cheese: this station it is onions. My Arabic is working well. They have just been telling the only French lady in the carriage that *everyone* in England speaks Arabic.

We are zigzagging up on a cog-wheel over stony hills, and all the olive stretches left between us and the sea. The country is terraced and bare now, its reddish earth lovely with blue shadows and ribbons of melting snow. People who want conversation stroll along the boards outside the carriages and look in at the windows. The sun is getting very hot already: it is the good burning sun of the hills up here. I have seen the first black Beduin tents pitched among poppies in the fields.

Later.

We are down across the ridge now in the flat valley between Lebanon and Anti-Lebanon: Hermon S.E. of us, looking less like a mountain than like the gentle culmination of his long ridge. It is good to see flat roofs instead of the horrid red tiles. And good to see people ploughing, and wide stretches of browny-green earth where corn grows, and poplar groves round the villages. A broad pebbly river-bed winds south: it might be Italy, only there is a camel. What an absurd silhouette they have! There seems to be little enough water about, but it is evidently a good soil for vines: they are not propped up, but stretched out flat with their branches outspread, like corpses on a battlefield, row upon row head downwards on the slopes.

At the top of the Pass, where there was a lot of snow, I saw a tank, its little gun and all complete, being used to clear the road: and another one further down. There was great snowballing at the stations. The passengers have kept reserves of snow to throw at unsuspecting labourers down here in the plain. The Syrian lady has just told me that she was blocked on the Pass seven years ago: the train could go neither back nor forth, and all the passengers had to spend six days in the little station building, for there is no village up there.

The party has got out now. Affectionate farewells. I thought we should be set alight in the long tunnel: we spent the time burning matches and dropping them casually about; when the little boy of three joined in the game I was really afraid for the woodwork. The Oriental attitude to women has been coming out very plainly. The poor little daughter could do nothing right; sit down; get up; don't do this: don't do that. But the son was allowed to slap his father's face and we all thought that a great joke.

We are now getting to the valley of the Barada: fantastic country. I will tell you from Damascus.

Did I tell you I saw an army of storks the other day, flying towards Turkey? Your FREYA.

65. *To her Mother.*

DAMASCUS. HOUSE OF KHALIL 'AID, BAB TUMA.
15.3.28.

DARLING B.,

I haven't been out yet, but the East has been coming home to me quite busily. Imagine one of those

little backyards in Venice as the entrance to my home.
You climb up rather rickety stairs, through the lower litter
of garments, saucepans, old shoes, and flower-pots to a
pleasant room with seven windows; where, unless you are
extremely careful, everyone can see you while you dress.
I really think the bed is all right: I didn't at first, but have
come to the conclusion it is only the greyness of home
washing. I have found nothing alive anyway: in fact
what I complain of is that everything smells as if it were
dead. The children's clothes were bundled out of my
room, and various necessities like jugs, towels, mirror, rug,
brought in at intervals while I sat rather dismal on the
bed. That has a lovely yellow quilt and two long hard
bolsters. I do manage to get hot water in the morning.
But there are so many smells.

I had breakfast with the family this morning and felt
how much I am still fettered to the lusts of the flesh.
Madame seems to dress in the eating-room and we had
to hunt for our food among her toilet things; all the debris
was thrown into a hole in the floor close by where the milk
is standing. We sit round the primus stove beside the
washing-up bucket, and I tried to anchor my mind on the
fact that nothing much besides old age can happen to the
inside of a boiled egg.

There is father, mother, aunt, and three girls—the only
ones to know any English in the family, and jolly children.
They asked me to join the evening circle last night, and
we sat in a bedroom with every window closed and received
two callers, a chauffeur and a policeman, whom I thought
objectionable. I wonder if I am getting fussy? The landlady is pretty and looks tired: her name is Rose: she is at
this moment blacking her eyes at my mirror; and she uses
my powder, which I do so dislike. If she did not wear
incredibly sloppy European clothes she would be quite
ornamental. There is no particular sort of privacy here,
except that the men are out of the way most of the time.
It will be splendid for my Arabic, and I believe I can
stand it. The best of it is a roof to walk about on and
look at the other roofs, and the minarets and the red hills.
The desert comes close; just red rock, not a shimmer of
grass on it: the cultivated land washes up to it like a

wave and stops as suddenly. It gives one the feeling of being in prison.

Later.

I have been out with Sitt Rose, and discovered a European side to the town, tramlines, avenues and shops: it is what they are proud of, of course.

I found Mr. P., the Vice-Consul, in that district. He was evidently so very pleased to have a new English person to talk to, but I did not like him very much. He has invited me to dinner, and to go walking, but I hardly think I shall do so. He does not know a single Syrian here. He thinks it impossible I should stay in my native lodging, but says there is no alternative except hotels.

The gardens of Damascus will soon be covered in fine dust. It has been blowing about all morning, squalls coming down from Hermon.

I was so glad of letters. I have been feeling a little depressed.

Your most loving FREYA.

66.   *To Lady Horlick, now Lady (Francis) Oppenheimer.*

DAMASCUS.   17.3.28.

DEAR LADY HORLICK,

This wobbly letter is from a bed of sickness in Damascus: not a long one I hope, for I think of being active again in a day or two. The prospect of being ill in a native household is too terrible.

I only came two days ago. A wonderful journey down the Barada valley; it is just a green strip between desert walls of red rock, as mad and fantastic as the landscape of dreams. You can take one stride from the rich garden land into the desolation. The valley suddenly opened, and there in the afternoon sun was Damascus, yellow as an opal, the river running through between straight banks like a willow-pattern plate. There is the exact description in Chaucer somewhere, of Simois "like an arrow clere" flowing through Troy, and I thought of it as I came along, and before the railway station turned the East to mere untidiness.

If I feel strong I hope to make journeys from here. It is all a question of food: you offend people if you refuse their hospitality, and you die (or I should) if you accept it. Perhaps you die in either case: I have not tried offending a Druse!

I have been introduced to a delightful Moslem Sheikh who will shew me Damascus free from tourists. He is part owner of the most beautiful house in the city and belongs to an old family of Albanian Turks who became Arabicised about four generations ago. I admired his good manners, for he came to call and was welcomed into my *bedroom* by the assembled family before my Arabic could rise to the occasion—before I had time for anything except to clutch the nearest dressing-gown. He sat talking with charming equanimity, though I am sure it is not the usual way in which to be introduced to a Moslem.

I was not able to reach Baghdad after all. Ja'far Pasha, who invited me, resigned, and is now sent as Minister to London.

I hope you will be somewhere near Venice in the summer? England seems far away.

My love to Betsan and much love and remembrance to you from

FREYA STARK.

67. *To Mrs. Aidan Thompson.*

DAMASCUS. 17.3.28.

DEAREST P.,

I am in Damascus. It is a wonderful fact—but I really am. Not however quite as I had expected, for I sickened as I came and after two days trying to bear up against my own inside and the first shock of life in a native household, I went to bed and sent for the English doctor.

I have no cupboard or drawer in my room, and the three children and my hostess sit on everything all day long—so you can imagine the chaos, me lying forlorn in very unbecoming pyjamas and no powder on my nose, when the aristocratic young Mohammedan to whom I have

an introduction walks upstairs.   Of course my Arabic was
inadequate for keeping him out, and my hostess flung the
door wide and greeted him with the pretty Arabic welcome
and no hesitation at all.   I had to make the best of it,
grabbing a stray garment and pretending to be happy.
I always seem to receive my Moslems in these unorthodox
ways: and such a handsome young man too.   I have to try
and get up for tea in his garden to-morrow, and will try
to look respectable.   We could not offer even coffee, for
it is still Ramadan, and he would not even smoke.   He
is one of the chief landowners here and owns many Druse
and Moslem villages, and practises with his uncle as a
doctor.   Most of the men of the family are condemned to
death and escaped out of the country, but he was out of
the trouble in the Sudan and does not enter into politics
now. I hope I shall be fit to enjoy life, for he suggests
devoting his afternoons to showing me the real East—and a
better East I rather think than my present impressions!

Some day I will upset your hygienic soul by telling you
exactly how one's meals are cooked here.   To my immense
relief I am ordered only milk and eggs and biscuits till I
get back to civilized Lebanon.   Otherwise I can bear it.
I pour my bath water (which is a basin) outside my bedroom door and it trickles somewhere into the blue through
a crack in the floor: the sanitation isn't worse than old-
fashioned Italy: and the family all wash on Saturdays,
even their hair.   My bed is fundamentally clean, and I have
seven windows to my room, two carved chairs, and one
divan to make up for the want of everything else.   And they
are all kind and friendly, and bring me flowers, and talk
with a pretty lilt that rises like the cadence to a song at the
end of every sentence and is peculiar to Damascus.   I must
say that when I came the first night, and simply curled up
with the results of Syrian food, and wandered up through
all the smells to my revolting meal, I felt the abyss of woe.
Do you know what a horrid sensation it is when everything
you touch wants cleaning?   The sun here must be a very
powerful disinfectant.   The three children are rather
nice, and they are the only things in the house that don't
look and smell as if they had died long ago.

Your loving FREYA.

68 *To her Mother.*

DAMASCUS. 17.3.28.

DARLING B.,

It is very annoying. I have been quite upset and ill. I tried to think it was imagination, but finally sent for the English doctor. Wonderful nation we are! He never asked a question, but gave me a prescription, talked about food (and well he might) to the lady of the house, and went. I was just longing for a little bit of moral comfort and felt this rather chilly. But I am glad it is nothing requiring energetic attention. I shall be all right living on leban and eggs.

My room is quite nice and quiet in itself, and the sun comes in. I get a cypress tree and bits of roof, and the children bring me flowers. The landlady comes to borrow stamps and envelopes. It is a relief not to have to see my food as it is being prepared; the leban looks tolerably white when I get it. Such a relief to have the doctor's authority for refusing everything else. I feel that it is rather hard on the poor people that their first European should be such a trouble. They are very obliging in their casual way. They come offering me raw salads to chew in bed as if I were a rabbit in a cage.

Luckily I got some books from the Mission. I dragged myself there to tea yesterday, but it was stuffy. They have a really charming house, painted rooms with mirrors let into the walls, and painted wooden ceilings: like good Venetian baroque. The court is paved with coloured marbles, and there is a red and white marble tank among lemon trees: at one side is a raised summer room they call the *dar*, open on one side, with divans and a table.

I will delay my letters a little so that when they reach you you will know I am all right.

Your FREYA.

69. *To her Mother.*

DAMASCUS. 18.3.28.

DARLING B.,

I am up again, languid but much better. I had to send a wire to V. (who has put off her coming till May) and reached the very edges of exasperation at the slowness. When the old man began *reading* my postcards before sticking the stamps on (with a queue of people waiting), I snatched them from him and gave a general shock to Oriental feelings.

To-day is Sunday and the family is fearfully smart: you would not have known them.

I have been wandering by Saladin's tomb, in a little garden of oranges and blossoming almond, with a marble fountain. My Sheikh took me, discussing religion. He likes me so much for not being a missionary. He told me that they do no harm because so far as he knew they have never succeeded in converting a Moslem: so that's that.

Your loving FREYA.

70. *To Miss Buddicom.*

DAMASCUS. 18.3.28.

DEAREST VENETIA,

I hope there may be no more telegrams, for it means an hour of irritation in this country to get them off. I have wired "Come May". It can't be helped but it is sad! It would be poor fun for you, however, to have me sick among the Druses, and I am rather uncertain of my own strength.

I don't like my landlady here. She borrows my soap, and whenever we are out together, she gets into a carriage which I have to pay for: and I dislike carriages anyway, because you never see anything but the coachman's back. The trouble with travellers—and this includes missionaries— is that they come into contact with only the third or fourth rate people, and that gives no impression of *any* country.

I am not going to say that my present family are typical
Damascus.

I have been to see some charming Mohammedans: a
young doctor and his sister (dressed in the latest French and
beautifully shingled). Their brother-in-law is a great
Nationalist, and was asked to speak to our legislators on
the Near East problems. The doctor took me out after
the call to look at Damascus outspread at our feet, its
groves of blossom stretching away to the hills in the sunset.
He swept his arm round one side of the landscape and said:
"This belongs to my family." It is wonderful rich land,
irrigated by the seven rivers, which lose themselves in
swamps full of duck and wild boars: all round are low
volcanic hills. In spite of dust, noise, tawdriness, ugliness
of detail, there is a magic: not to be understood in a day
or even two!

You won't put off your coming after May 1st, will you?
If I hurry to Lebanon and do not find you, I shall say
things, besides being brokenhearted.

Your loving FREYA.

71. *To her Father in Canada.*

DAMASCUS.   19.3.28.

DEAREST PIPS,

No news from you at the consulate, and I am so
anxious.

It is not all joy living with a native family. Meals, for
instance, are a trial: I am given a fork, but otherwise one
dips one's bread in the dish, and eats the most deadly food
swimming in every variety of fat. In the evenings we
sit in one of the bedrooms and hand round the hubble-
bubble. I have avoided that, however. My thoughts in
fact are beginning to concentrate quite morbidly on all
the things I might avoid.

What you would enjoy is sketching in the bazaars. I
thought them rather tawdry at first, with corrugated iron
roofs riddled with bullet holes of two years ago and filled
with semi-European shoddiness. But to-day I found my
way into the *Arabian Nights,* and it was very lifelike: sitting

on the ledges of the little open shops and buying silks which the merchant in his long gown spreads out before me, while the merchants opposite, squatting in *their* little shops, click their beads through their fingers like rosaries, and look at the rival transaction. The Moslem ladies have to lift their black veils so as to see the stuff they want to buy: you see them bending over, with one hand to the veil and the other holding up the garment for inspection: or trotting around with a bazaar porter behind them, a pile of packages on his head, just as the story has it.

The men are of many types: fair hill people; the real Assyrian; every degree of brown and black; Beduins in rags, swinging their rough cloaks with big strides, their dingy little tattooed womenfolk behind them; and many blue eyes with long noses and narrow foreheads, and a tired look about them as if life or the climate were too much for them: and perhaps it is. But there are fine rosy children about. Donkeys with panniers jostle in the crowd (sometimes with skins of oil, not at all pleasant to be near). Camels in long lines. Occasionally a splendid horse, with red and yellow trappings. And all in a half light, for the bazaars are roofed over, and the shops open on to them like dolls' houses about two feet off the ground—or like a row of boxes at the theatre.

I was much amused to see horses and donkeys clipped in patterns—their hindquarters arranged in lozenges and all sorts of delicate designs, according to the village they come from, says my sheikh.

My Sheikh took me about this afternoon, looking so well in his flowing gold and brown cloak that comes from Ibn Saud and the desert. We went through the narrowest back streets, arched over their own shadows, with slits of daylight dropping down on them like swords. They are like Liguria in a way, only the colour is different, baked to a creamy yellow. The flat roofs are just yellow mud solidified, delicious in tone; and there are delightful bits of black or red stone, or blue tiles here and there. It is extraordinary how little civilized beauty there is: nothing like the surprises and delights of any small Italian town. It is just a charm made up of sunlight and age.

A great piece of the town is still in ruins after the bombardment; such desolation: a whole district practically razed. The English are rather unfair, however, in saying they were not given warning: it seems that they were told beforehand, only as there had been two warnings already, and nothing to follow, they paid no attention. And now they say the shooting began without their knowing. So the missionaries tell me. I saw a poor little French lady trying to buy a blue ribbon for her baby, looking so forlorn among the strange hostile people. I offered her my Arabic (which begins to carry me nicely), and she was grateful: and I felt how horrid it must be to belong to an army of occupation. The suburbs as I came along the Barada valley are still all in ruins, and the place full of troops.

Your loving FREYA.

72. *To her Mother.*

DAMASCUS. 20.3.28.

DARLING B.,

B.B., whom I hadn't seen since Villa Trento, came through yesterday on her way to Teheran. I went to their hotel after dinner, and felt so overcome by the people there that I returned actually with relief to my own slum. B. and a friend want to go to Persia to take cinema pictures. Another friend was with them and remains a week in Damascus—an interesting young thing and very pretty. She is a Bahist, and staying with *the* Bahists at Haifa, the grandchildren of the Beha and present heads of the sect. She had a letter to one of the brothers here. When I came back to my room this afternoon I was surprised (slightly, for I am getting hardened) by seeing a man completely black sitting close to my washbasin. This turned out to be her friend, and she was there too, and the whole Rose family much interested but not pleased at this intimacy with Moslems. The Bahist was so charming that his blackness didn't matter: he only speaks Arabic, the flowery kind: I felt my replies were dreadfully matter of fact.

H

He has taken the young Bahist into his house and given her a beautiful clean room with food all to herself (for he and his wife can't eat in Ramadan), and she says she is going to be happy. How I wish I could leave the Christians and go there too. I am to call on Thursday. He is a tanner, and his name is Abd er Rahman or Servant of the Merciful: and he lives beside the Khan of the Melons, which is as near as you get to an address in Damascus. He was delighted when I mentioned Prof. E. G. Browne's name, and knew all about him. He was really a charming old man: I hope I shall see more of him.

Earlier in the afternoon, just as I was resting, Sitt Rose walked in with two Christian law students who came quite unasked to pay me a visit and whom I found very trying. I do dislike never knowing who is going to walk into my bedroom next. I was beginning to feel that perhaps I was fussy, but the expression of my Bahist—her name is Rosamund Wise—as she looked round, reassured me on that head. I think I shall make it a rule to avoid missionary recommendations in future.

Ramadan has just ended at sunset. Such a business in the bazaars, shopping for the feast. It lasts three days. We went on to the roof to hear the muezzin: it is extraordinarily moving, voice after voice ringing out from the high steeples to declare the greatness of God to the people below. The flat roofs of course give a wonderful advantage to the minarets. God is the *Master* here: not the Comrade and Teacher of our churches that stand clustered amid their flock.

Your loving FREYA.

73. *To her Mother.*

DAMASCUS. 21.3.28.

DARLING B.,

So cold again. The sun is hot and the wind icy, and I slept with Viva's rug *inside* my bed, all the windows shut, and a hot bottle.

The older lady has just been in to tell me tactfully that Moslems are not to be trusted. "Even if a Moslem smells like musk, do not put him into your pocket" was what she said. None of the people in this house smell like musk anyway. I have heard the same proverb quoted against Armenians. In fact I imagine it is useful in this country where everyone is against everybody.

I have been lazy this morning. First getting my knapsack ready in hopes of departing next week: and then sitting on the roof in the sun watching the domes, and the hills, and the beautiful cloud shadows, and Hermon's snowy shoulder. The light is lovely, so pure and brilliant: one feels it here as St. Augustine saw it, "that Queen of colours". There is nothing on these naked hills to interfere with its lovely play, and they change like water with the reflections of the sky.

We are going to see the entry of the Vizir: then I shall go for a country walk.

Yesterday I was asked if I was Arabic. It was only on the strength of two words, but imagine my joy.

Your own FREYA.

74. *To her Mother.*

DAMASCUS. 27.3.28.

DARLING B.,

I am going to get up to-day and try to get out. I seem much better and hope to be well by the end of the week—but I fear the donkey trip will have to be given up. It is heartbreaking, everything being propitious except my own self. I shall see if I can manage some small things from here, taking it easy with motors: but all the really interesting things can only be reached by riding and camping.

A kind American lady came yesterday and brought me soup: the first food I could eat with anything like pleasure these twelve days. I lapped it up, and was then prayed over, which was also kind and made me feel rather like the Deserving Poor. I thought it very nice of her, for my own missionaries who have got me into this house have neglected me completely, except for a few invitations to prayer meetings which are quite inappropriate when one is in bed with dysentery.

It is at last beginning to be warm. My room was 17 yesterday, and the terrace in the sun 27. But it is a climate full of tricks.

Perhaps you will realize the depths of my abasement when I tell you that last night I woke with the most violent irritation spreading all up my arms. "Ah," says I, "this is what is the matter with me! I have measles, or smallpox, or something." I turned on the light, and saw bites. "Is that all?" said I, and went to sleep again. To this am I reduced.

As a matter of fact I have not had any creatures so far. But the American lady depressed me, for she says that they come to you if you stay in bed; I saw in my mind a picture of long crawling lines drawing near over all the flat roofs of Damascus.

Cook's book just come. Thank you both so much. Oh how sick I am at the loss of my lovely trip. I have asked if I can meet Mr. Edmunds by car, and perhaps see one or two of the most accessible Hauran cities: but what a way of doing it!

I have just had a letter from Salehmy, really rather a touching letter, written with much care, and making me feel that my own was fearfully inadequate. Arabic is the grand language for pretty speeches.

Your own FREYA.

75. *To her Mother.*

DAMASCUS. 1 April 28.

DARLING B.,

This was intended to be posted to-day so as to reach you for your birthday with all my loving wishes, but I am again in bed, and so will keep it till I can send a satisfactory report. It is nothing serious, only as soon as I eat or move the trouble returns. How I wish one could do without eating in this world!

I had tea at the Mission yesterday, but did not go for a walk as intended, feeling too ill. I do find those ladies too suffocating. Even the young ones seem to have all natural interest in life and buoyancy taken out of them and think of nothing but their own narrow little bit of path of (self)righteousness. I have to use so much self-control not to say wrong things all the time, and even so they look on me as world and flesh if not actually devil.

They suffer from stagnation of the brain, and that surely produces stagnation of the soul in time. To feel, and think, and learn—learn always: surely that is being alive and young in the real sense. And most people seem to *want* to stagnate when they reach middle age. I hope I shall not become so, resenting ideas that are not my ideas, and seeing the world with all its changes and growth as a series of congealed formulas. When one sees even these *young* things with everything clearly immovable in compartments in their rudimentary minds, it is really depressing. They are not even like the busts on the Pincio, who at least had been *uomini vivi* before they were dead.

Well well. Good-bye.

Your loving FREYA.

76. *To her Mother.*

DAMASCUS. 2.4.28.

DARLING B.,

I am much better again to-day, and hope to be quite well by the end of the week. I was able to be out this morning and enjoy my walk through Damascus slums, trying to find the "four great gates". I had an adventure which might really make the mission hair stand up, and gave me a nasty qualm. I fell into it because it was so like the *Arabian Nights*. An old man with a venerable beard came up as I was strolling along with my camera, and said, just as anyone would expect: "Follow me, oh lady, and I will show you a beautiful place." So I followed. He told me it was an ancient bath, unused I supposed: and turned down a very narrow dark passage which went below the level of the street. I did hesitate, but he said "Have no fear," and it is not so easy as it seems to change one's course when once started.

We came to a heavy studded door, on which he knocked:
ten centuries dropped from me by magic: I should not
have been at all surprised to see the Caliph and his two
companions on the other side! The door was opened
from the inside, and there was a great vaulted hall, lighted
from a window in the roof, and with a cistern of flowing
water in the centre. There were alcoves with carpets on a
raised platform round three sides, and various men lying
about on them with their heads wrapped in turbans and
nothing much except their big bath wraps on. I did feel
I was not in at all a suitable place! They gathered round
me in an instant. Then I heard the door clank to behind
me with a horrid sound as if a chain were dropped.

I had an unpleasant sensation as if my heart were
falling—literally a sinking of the heart in fact—but I did
remain outwardly calm; only I put my back against the
wall so as to face them. I said to the old man: "Oh my
father, wilt thou hold my gloves while I take the picture?"
and got my camera ready with complete disregard to the
rules of photography. They had all come up so close to
me and I thought them a villainous-looking crowd. Someone murmured to the old man: "French?" "English,"
said I hastily: "we are your people's friends." This had
an extraordinarily soothing effect on the atmosphere. I
asked if they would mind moving away from me for the
picture, which they did in silence. When I had taken it
I thanked the man who seemed master of the bath and
turned to my old man to have the door unfastened: this
also was done in complete silence, but just as I was stepping
out two or three of them asked me to turn back and look
over the baths. This you may imagine I did not do. I
was very glad to have that door open, though I suppose it
was all really quite all right. I wish now I had taken the
picture with more care, for I don't imagine any European
has been in that particular place before. I am not mentioning this episode here, for as it is I am being almost
shadowed by the family, who are evidently fearfully
anxious. Think of it! My landlady has never in all her
life been even into the Great Mosque.

I finished the morning calling on my Bahist friends,
and found the mother and her little girls. Such a nice

woman. I gave Viva's ribbon to the little black girls
and they were pleased.

My Sheikh has taken me over the Great Mosque—a
wonderful, beautiful place to pray in. It was almost
as St. Marco for its atmosphere of peace. It is immense.
There is a great court, and portico of yellow marble, big as
a piazza and bathed in light, and you come into the twilight
under long rows of pillars dwindling away, in a beautiful
simplicity of unbroken walls. The richness and colour
is in the carpets. All the detail is lovely: the Imam's
niches, doors, pulpit, worked in marble and mother of
pearl, and old blue tiles outside under the columns: but
the general effect is absolutely simple; there is nothing
to take the eye or the thoughts away. The people wander
in to pray, or talk quietly. All the political plots were
hatched here. There are low platforms, where they read
the Koran, swaying backwards and forwards as they chant
it in a low voice. In one corner there is a marble basin
with flowing water. And there is a pleasant silence,
since everyone goes barefoot on the soft carpets. I should
like to spend hours there: and the Sheikh says no one would
trouble me if I did so.

If I go on improving so rapidly I shall take a day follow-
ing Barada—which is Abana—to where he loses himself
in his desert lake not far away.

Mr. Edmunds told me he would be here about the 8th,
but I have had no word since, and it is tiresome for it keeps
me here in uncertainty.

My dear love to you.

Your FREYA.

77. *To her Mother.*

DAMASCUS. 4.4.28.

DARLING B.,

Do you know that my living here comes to less than
6*s.* a day, and I am so rich I don't know what to do with
myself. My Sheikh won't let me spend it on motors for a
day or two as he is afraid of its shaking me too much.
It has really been useful to have a *slight* attack of dysentery,

for I have learnt a lot about its treatment, and especially about the injection to cure it, which I shall never be without now in places of this sort.

Yesterday we did no sight-seeing, but went up to Salahiye —my Sheikh and I—to look at Damascus in the sunset—her gardens getting greener day by day in the plain below. We met his cousin, H.E. Hakki Bey, a charming old man who was governor here four years ago. Chairs and coffee were brought us—all out in the open country, very pleasant. Two other gentlemen joined. His Excellency is going to Europe this year, and I asked him to come and see us if he goes by Venice. These well-bred Moslems are very agreeable, and just as easy to get on with as well-bred people the world over. Of course, one cannot become intimate unless one knows enough of their civilization to be able to see from their angle. If you think what we would be if we lost *all* our Latin and Greek roots together with their derivations, and substituted quite a different culture which most Europeans know only by name, you will see that one does not need a great divergence of character to explain the difficulty of understanding between East and West. I don't believe there is any more fundamental reason why one should not know a Syrian as intimately as anyone else who is not of one's own race. Another cause for misunderstanding is that the foreigner usually meets the lower classes here. *All* the people I would have met through the English in Damascus are small shopkeepers, or that sort.

I have most illuminating times discussing religion and politics with my Sheikh, and he talks quite freely, finding me interested. I told him that I have long thought of Mohammedanism as one form of Protestantism and far nearer to the spirit of Protestanism than the debased forms of Christianity here: and he seemed rather to like the idea. When he talks about such things his eyes light up, and he is quite different from his ordinary polite conversation.

He is convinced that the Koran is superior to the Bible, just as he is convinced that Arabic poetry is superior to the literatures of Europe. This is all interesting in someone who has been in the hands of the missionaries for the *whole* of his education. In fact I can't help feeling that my casual conversations are doing more for making an atmosphere of understanding than all their efforts put together, but this may be vanity. I do believe, however, that if they can only missionise among the lower classes they can do no good. Unless they can influence the sort of people who are going to govern and teach and generally run the country, they will never get any real influence at all.

I told my Sheikh about their alarms and warnings as to walking alone, much to his amusement: "I suppose they are afraid of being eaten by Moslems," said he. I asked him whether the Christians were disliked in Damascus. "Oh no," he said, "they never interfere, so we do not mind them." He tells me that the veiling of women is not a law but merely custom; the Koran permits one to shew face, hands and ankles. Miss H. here, while begging me not to visit alone at Moslem houses, said: "What can you feel about a religion where women are so degraded they cannot shew their faces?" So there you are.

As to politics, it is just as well not to say very much about them. I will tell you later. Miss Azm, the sister, told me a sad tale the other day of an agitated lady during the bombardment who was trying to hide her money, but in the distraction of the moment clutched the gold to her bosom and threw the baby down the well. I am not pro-French, but really felt that the High Commissioner couldn't be blamed for this. M. Ponsot, by the way, is here since yesterday, and the place is full of French officers. The Azms are invited to the reception, but not going.

Your own FREYA.

78. *To her Mother.*

DAMASCUS. 5.4.28.

DARLING B.,

Both your letters came together to-day—the first since those I found on arrival; something queer must happen *en route*. Anyway I was very glad to get them.

You will know by now that I am all right again, only vexed at the slowness of convalescing. I had thought of the hotel myself long ago, but the doctor advised me against it, now that my diet is reduced to leban. He says I am better here, where the people are kind, though casual. I begin to eat a little now, but only the very simplest things. If it were not that I don't know whether Mr. Edmunds is coming on the 8th or not, and have no means of getting at him to let him know, I should get out of the town altogether and recover at once in the country. If ever I live in an Eastern town again, I shall take just a room, and do my own cooking; I am sure that is the safest.

I am much relieved at a really cheerful letter from Pips. He is out pruning trees and does not want me till autumn. I was getting so worried about him. I hope you keep him supplied with books. I write when I can, but these days spend so much time *sleeping*: and I am at the mercy of anyone wandering in. Yesterday it was the two lodgers upstairs, and no one ever knocks! Even the cats push my door open to steal the dinner. I take credit to myself for not having yet seriously lost my temper, or at least not shewn that I lost it ! ! !

Your own FREYA.

79. *To Mrs. Jeyes*.

DAMASCUS.   5.4.28.

DEAREST VIVA,

I am so vexed at not having written all this while, thinking you would be travelling.

I am in love with the Enchanted City. It is nothing but a big oasis ringed with dead volcanoes of the desert. The streams rush into it and lose themselves eastward in the sand. Now it is all surrounded by young green leaves and fields of beans in flower or springing corn.

To-morrow my Sheikh, and his sister whose name is Handmaid of Allah, and Shahir his brother, and perhaps Brigand the retriever and the guns, are all going out with me, and we are going to try and find some ruins near the desert lakes. They are on my map, but no one seems to know much about them, and it rather depends if the country is such as the Ford can manage without a road. I have discovered a nice old chauffeur who is rather like a ruin himself, but takes his rattling old box over anything: there is an emancipated feeling with a car that will wander over cornfields: it ceases to be a machine.

I felt too weak for Arabic these weeks and have been enjoying a return to my native language, reading about the Druse massacres in 1860. I had no idea what a bloody affair it was, not unlike Cawnpore except that it was the men and not the women who were slaughtered: the Druses will let the women go, and those who were killed were killed by the Turks. They ended with a Moslem massacre of Christians here, and the total altogether was over 11,000 dead, and would have been more but for one of the chief Moslems who succeeded in saving thousands of Christians. I expect you know all this, but here it comes with great vividness, when one sees the actual sort of crowds that were engaged. The other day I saw a French coloured regiment marching through the town with band playing, and was watching the people as they turned to look back at it, and could not help seeing that they looked very much as if they would like to begin again. I must keep off politics however.

You will have had my news in Asolo, and have heard that I am being well looked after by swarms of missionary ladies who keep on telling me what I MUSTN'T ... I have obstinately continued to consort with Mohammedans, and this has caused a slight coolness. It seems that the Mohammedans spit at them—but they do nothing so unpleasant to me, and the only people I have ever had to snub are Christians!

It is a leisurely land. Everyone has time to talk, everyone is ready to be interested: it is only when you want to get anything done that you begin to be unhappy. To buy a dressing-gown is pure Romance. You sit on the ledge of a little shop and the merchant spreads his wares: an audience gathers, and advises: the money-changer comes along to help. Then you bargain. You are told that the thought of profit does not enter with One whose face is like the Moon: whereupon you offer half. Then the diplomatic merchant says that he knows you are "a daughter of the Arabs": and who would refuse him anything after that?

I am not learning much Arabic here, but a great deal about Oriental life in general. Next week I shall learn nothing at all, for an Englishman from Brumana is to be here, and I shall just have a holiday and abandon my Sheikh. And I wonder if that will please the Mission any more? It is a kind dispensation that there should be so many pleasant people in Asia.

Ever your own FREYA.

80.   *To Miss Penelope Ker.*

DAMASCUS. 7.4.28.

DEAREST PEN,

P. will have told you that I foolishly picked up a malady that has left me tired. The riding will have to be given up—not so much because of riding in itself, but because I could not carry sufficient water, and Druse wells are all more or less poison.

Yesterday was a wonderful day: for I discovered the Desert!

One must not believe people when they tell you things. They told me I could not see desert unless I went to Palmyra which is too far this time. I looked at the map, however, and decided on a lonely ruin marked where the Damascus streams lose themselves in lakes, and the villages end. Nothing beyond but names of hills and water-places and the Road of the Raiders trailing away South to the lands beyond Jordan. My Moslem friends came with me bringing their guns, which we had to hide whenever police came in sight. The pretty sister wears a black veil over her face, but she throws it back in the country.

Such a road! It was sandy and smooth at first, running through avenues of walnut just coming into leaf, and the green corn on either hand. Then we began to wade streams, water well up to the axles: then on to banks at absurd angles. We began to meet Beduin: their black tents were dotted here and there. The country got poorer, the corn thin and uneven, the trees stopped. For some time there would still be a clump of shade by the villages—then nothing—just the mud walls baked yellow sloping up one of the strange solitary little hills that rise out of all this country like dolphins' backs.

When we reached the last village we had an affair to get a guide: they were all afraid we should abandon them in the wilderness. My Sheikh told me he sometimes has to take them by force, and once a man threw himself out of the car and nearly killed himself. Luckily persuasion did it this time. We were taken along a road that melted into invisibility, then found ourselves on hard sand, thorns and desert rushes brushing against the wheels. The country looked white like chalk here, all gentle lines and travelling shadows; and, half lost in distance, a glimmer of snow from Hermon, and the Damascus hills.

And then the wonder happened! Camels appeared on our left hand: first a few here and there, then more and more, till the whole herd came browsing along, five hundred or more. I got out and went among them to photograph. The two Beduin leaders, dressed gorgeously, perched high up and swinging slowly with the movement of their beasts, shouted out to me, but the Beduin Arabic is beyond me. I can't tell you what a wonderful sight it was: as if one were suddenly in the very morning of the world among the people of Abraham or Jacob. The great gentle creatures came browsing and moving and pausing, rolling gently over the landscape like a brown wave just a little browner than the desert that carried it. Their huge legs rose up all round me like columns; the foals were frisking about: the herdsmen rode here and there. I stood in a kind of ecstasy among them. It seemed as if they were not so much moving as flowing along, with something indescribably fresh and peaceful and free about it all, as if the struggle of all these thousands of years had never been, since first they started wandering. I never imagined that my first sight of the desert would come with such a shock of beauty and enslave me right away. But I left it feeling that somehow, some time, I must see more of the great spaces.

We had much more during the day. Shooting by the lake: losing our guide: then a really adventurous bit of cross-country motoring, as it were over heather, only here it was a kind of wormwood with a strong aromatic scent.

We found an old ruin surrounded by some poor Arab graves and Emptiness all about. The wind howled down so that one could scarce stand outside the lee of the wall: there was no water visible anywhere, except the brackish whiteness of the lake in the distance: and no tree in sight: nothing to break the horizon except the sudden weird little hills. The nearer landscape was brown like heather, though here it was really the colour of the hard soil shewing through scrubby little plants. Here and there there were heaps of stones, possibly old walls and houses, but quite indistinguishable.

Let me hear from you in Brumana. And love to you both always from

FREYA.

81.   *To her Father*.

DAMASCUS.   7.4.28.

DEAREST PIPS,

I had my first whole day out yesterday for a long time: and a good day too, nine and a half hours motoring or walking, and the motor was the harder exercise. We didn't bother about roads, but went into the scrubby desert. All the chauffeur drew the line at was marshes, and when we came to a hill full of loose boulders, very like Wild Tor, it was we who refused to allow him to attempt it, and got out and walked.

My friends are splendid at picnics. The Handmaid of Allah sees to the lunch-basket. The two boys bring their guns and the dog. We made for the lake: "The Little Sea of Hijane" is its name, and there are lots of duck—but not a rush to hide behind. We found no duck, however: indeed it was only by collaring a guide at Hijane village that we found the lake, for it is an hour without a road and the white water hardly shews in the white soil. I don't quite know what the trouble was with the guide. He was a wild-looking fellow with an old military coat looted off a German and a ragged white muffler round his face held on with one of those black camelhair fillets which seem to be clapped on at any angle and never slip off.

My Sheikh didn't seem over-confident, for he told me in his crisp English: "This man will not play tricks, for if he does I will beat him. And now when we leave the car I will see if he has a revolver." As the poor man was only one to five I did not feel much alarm. But as we were walking to the lake, the Handmaid of Allah murmured to her brother: "Would it not be better to make the guide walk in front?" and went on to tell me that her cousin had been killed by having his guide behind him—a Druse too and an ally during the rebellion.

The lake is shallow and there were flocks of white birds with slender wings, so beautiful, Shahir flung himself into the water to the waist, forgetting this world and the next in his eagerness. They shot them flying high, their wings catching the sun. I did wish they could escape. When one came down the others hovered over the place of its fall with a sweet shrill song. It seemed a great shame. We got also thirteen small partridges and another desert bird. Both the men are excellent shots and fearfully excited over it: and one does feel in this country that a gun is a useful object.

We came near to the village again on our way to my ruin, and here the guide deserted. I don't know what happened, for I wasn't attending till I heard the Sheikh call him an Animal, and a Creeping Creature, and saw him stalking off with great dignity. They wouldn't tell me what it was about, but I noticed we took the back road round the village on our way home.

What with the map and the desert road we thought we could find the ruin for ourselves. The road is just a bit of wilderness cleared of scrub and marked with two lines of stones like a diminished Dartmoor Avenue. In fact the *feeling* of the landscape was very like Dartmoor, before the heather shews anything but brown. The place of the Tors is taken by sudden little volcanic mounds—Tells— thick as mushrooms. We saw our citadel from far away on top of one of them: and it went on being far away. A horrid barren wind began to blow, lashing furiously. We made across country, going gingerly, for there were rushes and we didn't want to stick with nothing but the inhabitants of an unfriendly village anywhere near.

At last we came to the ruin and climbed up over the stones, and had lunch in its shelter. The others were all disappointed, for there was not an inscription nor anything of special interest. But I was happy enough. There was enough for the imagination; the old fort quite square, built of solid black stones without mortar; an entrance opening to one large central room, and four smaller rooms on either side. It cannot have been more than one story high, and outside was a rubble of stones out of which wandering Beduins had built a number of rough graves, like Druid circles. You looked out on to a great space, treeless, free as air. At the back the Raiders' Road— "so called from its insecurity" my guide book says—runs invisibly between its dotted stones into the waste lands. I wondered what the Roman garrison thought of it, and whether they used to grow their salads and tomatoes on the sunny side of the hill, and how they lived. Our own lunch got covered with sand as fast as we could eat it, but it was good. I was glad of my fur coat. In Damascus the temperature has been 20 centigrade in the shade all this time. Never shall I travel in the East without a big coat at *any* season.

I tried to get pictures, but there was little sun. The villages are a delicious colour, baked like the ground they are built on, all low walls, and no windows to speak of. The women were all out on the bare space outside the villages making solid dung cakes and piling them in the sun for winter fuel. It is all they can get except for some gnarled roots we saw being carried in on donkeys from the desert, a long way out.

I think you had better write to Asolo after you get this.

Your loving FREYA.

82. *To her Mother.*

DAMASCUS. Monday, 9.4.28.

DARLING B.,

I had just given up Mr. Edmunds and made up my mind for a lovely four days' trip towards Leja and Bashan, when I got news of him, aggravatingly saying he will come *either* to-morrow or Thursday—apparently oblivious that I may want to do something besides wait for his charming presence. I suppose it is not bad for my health to be quiet, though so dull. I can't tell you how bored I am with the poems of Browning, and I have read through the whole of Dante. He, Mr. E., does not tell me how he arrives, so I can't meet him and he will have to go and ask for me at the mission; and I can't order a room for him at the hotel without knowing the day: and I wonder if it is exactly correct for him to stay here? These niceties are beyond me.

My landlady has come with an astonishing request. She wants me to let her know whether there is anywhere in Italy where Yvonne, the child of fourteen, could be trained as a nurse, and what the conditions are? I wonder if you could find out? Nurses are sadly wanted here, and I suppose Yvonne might learn to eat with a fork and to wash at more regular intervals. She is a nice child, and some sort of regular training might be the making of her. Poor people! My landlady told me she was married at thirteen and had to learn everything afterwards. The trouble is that she thinks she *has* learnt everything! She asked me if I thought the Consul would send friends of his here as lodgers. I can see them trying to dismember their luncheons with a teaspoon and pocket-knife!

LATER.

I have had a long visit from my Sheikh, very excited over a tragedy that happened about a fortnight since. An American girl was living at a school kept here by an elderly Russian lady, who seems rather wanting in scruple. My friends had been kind to this girl, introduced her to a cousin of theirs whose wife shewed her all sorts of kindness and hospitality and often had her in the house. She has now run off with the cousin, and he has written to say he is divorcing his wife, and the whole family is to be broken up. The Russian lady seems a peculiar sort of head-mistress: she used to invite the French officers to dance and drink champagne with her Mohammedan pupils! and apparently knew all that was going on in this affair. It is rather disgusting. A few such things might explain

I

a lot of anti-European feeling. I told the story to Sitt Marie, the Aunt here, and got the unexpected conclusion from her that "this comes of dealing with Muslems". When I said that this was probably just what they were thinking about the Christians, she looked at me with sorrow. But she is a genuine Christian, and loves me with the tenderness reserved for straying goatlets.

I am learning how necessary it is to keep one's own standards and one's national standards for one's own use, and not to judge other people by them. My Sheikh said: "When we thought this Russian teacher was not what we had imagined her to be, we set spies on her among the servants, and they saw terrible things (with a wave of the hand quite beyond words) *through the keyhole*!"

Another thing I have noticed is the absolute lack of all historical sense among these people. No *perspective*. What happened five hundred years ago has the exact vividness of yesterday. It came upon me with a shock when a child here was reading out some of the more gruesome massacres in Kings: I decided on the spot that I should leave the Old Testament out of the curriculum if I were a missionary, and stick to Christian charity and the New. If you come to think of it, the Old Testament is the worst literature possible for these races: with that on the one hand and the Koran on the other the reign of toleration has very little chance.

Your own FREYA.

83. *To her Mother.*

DAMASCUS. 11.4.28.

DEAREST B.,

We had solemn farewells yesterday at the Sheikh's house. I came at an inconvenient moment, just when the young people's mother was taking up all the drawing-room floor for her prayers, and we had to step round her. She was such an intelligent-looking little lady, and sent her greetings to you. Her hair was slightly dyed with henna, and she spoke only Arabic.

I took a little present to the girl, and was given a terrible production of her own in return, blue paint on pink georgette—you will see! Alas! European art! They showed me their paintings, copied from celebrated pictures with a disastrous competence; so that I felt they had much better stick to the Moslem law against reproducing the human form.

The Sheikh came with me afterwards to choose a knife. We got one with a fine gay handle and a wicked point—the shopkeeper much impressed at dealing with an expert when he expected a tourist. The result was that I paid 20 instead of 100 lire. I refused to accept it as a present, having already received an offering of scent at the street corner where a man from Basra sits with a yellow turban and a tray full of little flagons in front of him. I chose musk in a little gilt case. I think I must bring David some.

After the shopping, we explored two mosques, full of green and blue tiles. Anything more beautiful than these old tiles it is impossible to imagine, and the interiors of the mosques are delightful, too; places full of peace and pleasant in atmosphere.

Mr. Edmunds will, I imagine, turn up to-morrow evening and I am trying to cure my cold and not look too swollen in the face, for his benefit.

I wandered into an old dyers' place yesterday, underground with an immense vaulted roof, and the inmates with their hands stained indigo, and big turbans. They were very amiable.

A sad tragedy. All my photos on the day of the desert are bad: there was no sun, and the terrific wind shook the camera.

Your own FREYA.

84. *To her Mother.*

BRUMANA. Tuesday, 17.4.28.

DARLING B.,

Before telling you of these last days, I must explain how I come to be home again with Miss Audi. On Thursday Mr. Edmunds arrived: his voice mingled in my afternoon dreams, and I rushed down more or less completely dressed so as to save him from being launched unprepared into the horrors of the family's sitting-room. I was more glad than I can tell you to see a normal human being of my own kind again! It was rather amusing: M. Paul Alexandre chose the same afternoon to appear unexpected on my doorstep. The two gentlemen's unhesitating verdict was that my lodging was Impossible, and they urged me to return in their car: I was in that state of feeble imbecility when the one thing that one cannot do is to make up one's own mind: so I let it all be done for me, and am really so grateful to them. It is only now that the effort is over that I realize how great it was!

My Damascus home was really rather unspeakable. Poor Mr. Edmunds! He bore up very creditably, but he will never know how much, *much* worse it might have been: I went upstairs when they were supposed to have prepared his room up on the roof, and made them do it all over again from the beginning, initiating them into the mysteries of washing down a floor. And I kept him carefully out of the dining-room, which was enough to make a quite strong man faint away. Even so, "much remained to conquer still"; under the present conventions of polite language we could not discuss the most peculiar peculiarities; a curious expression comes over his face whenever we come anywhere near the subject, however. I think he was a little overcome when I put my precious sprayer, carefully filled with Keating's, in his hand as a good-night offering. Never have I done such a thing to a young man before; I felt strongly that it was East of Suez.

M. Paul was rather a bore because it meant that I had to speak French, English and Arabic alternately all day long, and also he gravitated irrepressibly to all that was European and seemed to be drawn by a magnet to things like tramlines. And I had to bargain for such atrocious objects on which he set his heart. We spent a morning in the bazaars. The two were just like infants buying new toys; I enjoyed it so much.

After lunch we were firm with M. Paul, and packed him, all beautifully dressed in city black, into a little carriage and took him into the country and set him down

near a little copse by a stream and made tea. Sitt Rose
had forgotten the milk : a convenient sheep near-by provided
us ; the fellah milked her into our tea cup, and then strolled
up and talked to us with more members of the family—
pleasant people they were, so courteous and hospitable.
We walked back through a green and peaceful country,
poplars and walnuts and blossoming pear trees, the evening
coming on and cattle returning from the fields. We
passed through my village, where I had so flustered the
Mission by walking alone, and found the people sitting in
circles outside their doors in the cool light, the women
going to the stream with their pitchers. The people from
whom I had bought leban recognized me with smiles and
greetings : it was all friendliness and pleasant manners,
and all so lovely in the soft twilight. There seems to be
something peculiarly luminous in the air of Damascus—
as if the atmosphere were thinner than elsewhere and the
light could shine through more easily.

Next day was more or less taken up by business. I had
to pack, and pay good-bye calls. I went out a little with
Mr. Edmunds, and we strolled about among the little
shops, watching their crafts : the tinsmith polishing his
coppers by standing *in* them on a pile of wet gravel and
then twirling himself from side to side at such speed that
the gravel polishes off every stain in no time. Then the
weavers weaving striped silk for waistcoats—a nice Mohammedan with a beard. Then the man who presses tarbooshes
under a heavy brass press heated by a primus stove. Then
the man who lives in a little dark shop cooking rice in milk
all day long. Then the makers of sabots; they chop
them neatly out of pieces of tree trunk with hatchets, and
give them their slim shape with a couple of clever strokes.
Then we wandered into the jewellers' *suq*—a gloomy place
they lock at night, and filled with great iron safes. By this
time it was too late to do any orthodox sight-seeing.

On the Sunday, our last day, we went out to the lake
where Barada ends. Luck again : for we found the Beduins.
It really was a good day all through. We had two absurd
little Christians to drive us, with faces like the wooden

soldiers in *Chauves-Souris* : we liked them better as the day
wore on and they forgot to worry about the health of their
car whenever we came to a ditch. We did get rather
involved in ditches and ploughed land and stretches of
water after we left the last village. Then Providence came
along in the shape of a sprite of a boy, full of enterprise and
adventure, with a lovely Arab profile and flashing eyes.
He must have had the pure Arab in him somewhere, for
all he was a fellah of the village. He ran like a greyhound
under his clumsy bundle of clothes. He clambered on to our
car and showed us the way without our ever asking him,
and led us among the waterways at acute angles till we
reached the grassland and all was easy going.

The Beduin black tents were dotted round. It was a
happy place ; open sky and the river moving slowly, quite
deep, through the grassy plain. Our boy waded across,
walked up to a meditative family of donkeys, and came
back riding, with nothing but Mr. Edmunds's stick to help
him. I longed to see Beduins : Mr. E., very superior,
having seen many in Palestine, was not encouraging :
M. Paul looked dubious over the river. I mounted,
however, and Mohammed behind me, and we got across,
and the donkeys were whacked back into the stream for
the two gentlemen to seize and make the most of, which
they did. The Beduins came towards us and we strolled
to the tents. I think I was well inspired : I asked for the
Sheikh's tent, and this seemed to be the right thing : it
was the biggest of them all, open along the front and
divided into wattled compartments, and we were taken
to the largest compartment where the two coffee pots
stood in a hole in the ground and the sheikh himself lay
fast asleep beside them. In a corner at one end all the
tiny lambs were huddled safely.

A rug was spread for us : we squatted down, and looked
across at our sleeping host, who began to come to himself
very gradually. Mr. Edmunds considers that he did it
with great dignity, but I was feeling slightly nervous as
to my unsupported Arabic (M. Paul knows a few words, but
they usually say something he doesn't intend). The Sheikh
finally came to a sitting posture, in which he remained
meditative for a while with his eyes on the ground, looking

magnificent in his flowing garments and grey beard. He then spat, reached out a hand to the man nearest him—a fierce long faced Arab with two long pigtails—and began murmuring in quite incomprehensible language which did not sound particularly cordial. I made a feeble attempt at explaining our existence, but one can't carry on small talk with a Patriarch, and the correct thing seemed to be to sit silent, which we did for some time.

After a long while, the Sheikh stretched his hand to the coffee pot, and poured out a few sips into two little cups which he handed to me and M. Paul (I was surprised at the woman being first served!). Another problem: was one to drink it all, or leave some in the cup? One ought to know these formalities before wandering. I left some, and seemed to have done the wrong thing, for the Sheikh looked at it with awful intentness and finally poured it away on the ground, and gave me no more; which was a pity, for it was so good. M. Paul then offended very seriously by refusing the cigarette which the kind A.D.C. had (literally) just licked into shape for him. He made it up by offering his tobacco pouch, and the atmosphere began to thaw. "Oh daughter of my heart," said the old Sheikh to some question of mine: after that I felt all must be well.

I went and sat a little among the women in the next compartment and was warmly welcomed there. They were much interested in my clothes and tremendously impressed by silk knickers. I looked at their thick saddle bags and weavings. It seemed a good deal cleaner than my Damascus home. The women were charming: one or two truly beautiful, with small, delicate straight features: every movement was graceful and full of ease and dignity. They are tattooed all over their chins up to the lower lip, and their head-dress is of the same colour, and wraps the face round like a nun's: and the whole effect with the long blue gowns and silver bracelets is very dignified and beautiful. They were pleased with my name: I pronounced it Faraia, and it is very like one of the Arab names. It was a joy to hear the beautiful language well spoken. I believe it is only in the desert you can hear it so. I was also pleased at being able to understand so much.

Our motor meanwhile somehow found its way round the river and came lumbering up looking remarkably incongruous. We were able to get at chocolate and distribute it round, though I noticed no one ate till we gave the good example. We were now conversing. They told us of their wanderings. In winter they find grazing five or six days' journey in the desert: the old sheikh told me the land there is full of ruined cities. Finally, as we got up to go, they said they were preparing our meal. This was an awful prospect: certain death for me, anyway. I explained that we had already eaten the meal in our hearts, but that we must get round the lake before nightfall and could not wait, but would eat the fatted sheep next time. This was a brilliant linguistic effort, and successful. They watched us into our car with interest, but no vulgar curiosity. I ventured on a joke and told the sheikh that our camel ate more than theirs, and got a charming smile out of him: he was a beautiful old man, with a head meant for Leonardo or Michelangelo to copy, and kind eyes.

That was the best of the day, though the rest was good enough. We skirted the rushes, the lake full of herons and duck and innumerable strange birds catching the sun on coppery wings. The space was immense! We lunched in the shadow of the car with the warm wind singing round us. To the north and east, small sandstorms were whirling along in high columns: and we saw mirage, blue waters so unmistakable that we were taken in. We made tea under difficulties, trying to keep the wind off the saucepan and the dust out of the drink, not very successfully: and finally came home in the late evening light along the Palmyra road. In spite of all, Damascus has been well worth while.

Yesterday we came away—a lovely drive by the green Barada water, then high along the desolate ridge of Anti-Lebanon, all red earth and rubble, with Hermon on our left striped with snow. Then a sudden glorious descent, very steep, into the broad flats of Beqa with round green hills rising like islands; and Lebanon on the opposite side, also striped with snow and descending in great red folds: absurd colours, like Dolomites, only more violent. I shall never forget Hermon as we climbed and looked across the green spaces to where he lay like a great wave asleep in the sun crested with white. We climbed into the crisp air, good breath of hills reached snow: here they have built houses to pack it for Beirut's summer ices. Here one looked over half Syria, and we tried to induce M. Paul to lunch like an Olympian, but he wanted Hammana down the other side, and orgies of Victorian sentiment where Lamartine wrote platitudes about that tiresome Jocelyne. So we lunched among the Lebanon pines, feeling very much like coming home.

We have left the East behind us. This is not Europe: but it is Mediterranean, the same family as Villatella or Greece. Very lovely. A thin film of very vivid green from young corn and mulberry leaves is over it all. The last snow just melted off Sannin.

Miss Audi embraced me. And gave me a bath. You never saw anything so immaculate as my bed-curtains! I found myself *stroking* their lovely whiteness!

Your own FREYA.

85. *To Mrs. Jeyes.*

BRUMANA.   18.4.28.

DEAREST VIVA,

I have left Damascus. In spite of all I still carry the Enchanted City in my heart. We had one scrumptious breakfast in the hotel lounge before leaving, but even while revelling in the softness of those cushioned chairs, I could not help pitying all the poor misguided tourists from the very bottom of my heart!

My second day in the desert was even better than the first. We had coffee with a Beduin Sheikh—Ghassan of the Rualla was the name, I think. We found ourselves sitting there without having thought about it beforehand, on a nice mat on the ground with three chief Arabs sitting opposite and the coffee pots between us: all silent. The two older men were really magnificent, their manners perfect, their long trailing sleeves and draped heads under the black fillets immensely dignified. It was impressive: and might have been 4,000 years ago. I don't know what they made of us, but it all became very friendly before we left. The last we saw was the whole family gathered together, one man keeping the flock of sheep back from our car, the tall figures standing with an indescribable grace on the short desert grass. It alone was worth three years Arabic: like looking through a window on to a life completely unknown, and strange and beautiful from its fitness: an immense sense, too, of space and freedom. It was a shock later in the day, when we had rounded the lake and were running at a fine pace over the hard sandy earth, to see another car and be told it was the son of the Sheikh Nuri Sharlan returning to his tribe!

I have discovered that it is easier to be made welcome without a man around in this country. I went with Mr. Edmunds through the lovely emptiness of the Great Mosque before leaving Damascus, and had a very different reception from last time. A fierce old Hajji in green turban came growling for baksheesh and took us sullenly round, till I asked him about his pilgrimage to Mecca. Then he melted slightly as far as I was concerned and told me he was one of the Serif, of the Prophet's family, and shook hands when we left, though I don't think his kindness extended to Mr. Edmunds.

Lebanon is delicious now and I am warm. I mean warm for the day, not just for an hour to be chilled the next. I am busy trying to get fat again.

Your loving FREYA.

86.   *To Miss Buddicom.*

BRUMANA.   20.4.28.

DEAREST VENETIA,

Joy to get your letter. I can't tell you how I long for May 1st. I will go down to Beirut, and fetch you up in the evening.

No, I have no fixed plans. I have had bad luck—dysentery in Damascus. Syrian ladies in rows sitting round the bed eating candied oranges over my languid body; wandering strangers coming in to ask after me (as no one undresses they think nothing of bedrooms. They attributed my illness to my queer habit of taking my clothes off at night). My Moslem doctor pulled me through. He is a good man, and so nice. And has refused to let me pay him for all his work. I am beginning to feel less miserably weak now and may yet be fit for the rock cities if you can bear the heat. It is all black basalt and no trees, but would be a fascinating thing to do.

I had two days in the desert: only the fringe of course, but yet it was freedom, limitless more than the sea, for you felt no shore to it. Oh, indescribable. I saw a Beduin waving to his horse and the creature come to him from quite a distance, galloping, a beautiful sight. If you wave your sleeve (they wear very long trailing ones), it is a sign of friendship: this man made us the signal, a draped figure standing in that loneliness as our car jolted over the rough ground. One can hardly believe all this is Real Life and not mere Literature! We found a Roman fort, nothing of it left but walls, still square and sharp, the big stones laid without mortar, the waste lands round it. Behind us and already out of sight ran the last eastern road, old as the Druids and trodden always by people on the watch: no peaceful harvests or leisurely strolling there. The wind was howling and buffeting, with clouds scudding along, making the landscape soft as a moorland, though it was nothing but wormwood and baked earth. We ate our food with little clouds of Roman sand blown off the hewn stones and thought of the fragility of things.

I shall not write again but just expect you.

Your loving FREYA.

87. *To her Mother.*

BRUMANA. 21.4.28.

DARLING B.,

I am still revelling in the bliss of idleness in a nice clean house. Am looking a regenerated creature too and getting fat. I told Mr. Edmunds that my gratitude for being torn from Damascus would last a week and then I would begin to repine: so he came round last night to see if the change was beginning, and told me of the fearful shock Brumana got when it heard that we had been, so to speak, staying together in that villainous house. M. Paul, with true delicacy, had given out that they were together at the hotel, and Mr. E. waited till the middle of a dinner-party at the Fox's to mention casually where he was lodged, and watched poor Mr. Fox getting pink in the face. They are really nice people: they all seem to have stood the shock and are rather nicer to me than before.

The Fox's have also been telling him that we were lucky with our Beduins and that poor Miss H., who is an amiable lady, somewhat plain, was robbed of everything except one garment which she managed with difficulty to persuade them to leave her. I am so glad I did not have to come home with the two gentlemen in my chemise.

My Arabic has done well in Damascus. I was too ill to work and thought no progress was being made, but find that it has been sinking in of itself and that I know much more than I did. I think I can now travel about quite happily, and could even do interpreting if it came my way. It is only if I got into any sort of tight corner that my language would not do for getting me out again.

I saw Najm, the Druse guide, looking so active and intelligent, striding along with a black silk head-dress tied round his tarboosh and all the tassels waving, and a gun slung behind him. It gave me a pang! I must have at least a couple of days with him before we leave.

Poor Mlle., who is composed of sentiment and softness and simply pining for romance, cannot understand how I can come home with a charming young man under these intriguing circumstances, and yet eat my meals with quite an ordinary appetite. "*Nous sommes plus tendres que cela,*" says she, looking unutterable. I told her that I thought it would be most indelicate to be "tendre" *first,* and that she had better look for the incipient symptoms in the gentleman when next he comes to dinner.

They have just had a missionary conference in Jerusalem which has annoyed the Moslems and caused riots and protests all over the country. The irony is that the local Christians have joined in the Moslem protests. The Government must bless them all.

Ever so much love, darling B.   Your FREYA.

88.   *To her Mother.*

BRUMANA.   30.4.28.

DARLING B.,

Venetia arrives to-morrow, and I shall keep this to add news of our plans as soon as we can make them.

After lasting for nine days the sirocco has gone, and I had a long walk on Friday in a soft damp mist which seemed all out of place in this landscape. It made the flowers look very bright and I found quantities—dog rose and hawthorn, cystus and orchids, and many strange ones. My legs still carried me very feebly: I must get them into training for V. I don't think we shall wait here long: she will not be able to stand the gramophone for one thing. Mlle. has a new sentimental disc which is nearly driving me silly.

It is high time I left. I had a delightful Sunday out with Mr. Edmunds yesterday, but we counted that it was the fourth spent in some reprehensible way that meant absence from Church! Mr. Fox dares not remonstrate for he leans on Mr. E. for the whole management of his school, but it must be a strain, not to mention the feelings of the rest of Brumana.

We found a lovely walk. Took the car to where the road cuts the valley and stream and then followed up the water—a gentle stream with pools and ripples, and the valley wide and like a cup for sunlight, coming down in pine ridges, range upon range, with something of a park about it, and something Arcadian. One went on and on round each corner, impossible to stop. We found a little side valley for lunch, and made salad and cooked the coffee, and then strolled down to the river to wash up and sat and looked at the water, which is always the most entrancing occupation in the world: and then found patches of cool pine-tree shadow to fall asleep in (I did anyway); and then made tea, and found we could not reach our car again till forty minutes after time and could only just manage to be home in decent time for supper. It was the most beautiful valley I have yet seen here; so remote, and yet friendly, for there was an old bridge, half ruined, and vines and olives here and there, and just a house or two—exactly like the old romances. It was a happy day altogether.

Brumana school went down to Beirut for sports on Saturday and Mr. Edmunds gave me an entertaining account of the Syrian ideas of play. One of his best runners suddenly dropped out for no reason except that he had five boys in front of him and said he could never run in a race unless he were leading. Another missed his entry because he was not attending when his name was called. Brumana now has quite a creditable football team, thanks to great energy and hard work on Mr. E.'s part, but the opposing team spent their time trying to kick the adversaries instead of the ball. One of our poor little boys remonstrated while his shins were being kicked and was told that he would be killed if he said any more about it!

Your own FREYA.

89. *To her Mother.*

BRUMANA. 3.5.28.

DARLING B.,

Venetia is here, looking very thin but pretty. It is good to have her. We shall be leaving the day after to-morrow, and wandering, and only know that we must reach Jerusalem by May 20th. I hope for letters there.

Crowds of people coming to say good-bye. I feel it hard to believe that in two days' time Brumana will be in the past.

Love to you from

FREYA.

The two friends go by car to Baalbek and Damascus. Their next expedition is an unconventional and adventurous one, seeing that the Druse revolt of August, 1925, had continued until March, 1927, and that the French rulers of Syria were far from welcoming intruders. They are mounted on donkeys and with a Druse guide called Najm make a leisurely progress towards Palestine. At the end of eleven days they are at Bosra. There they dismiss their guide and take a car for Jericho and Jerusalem.

The sequel is not told in the letters, but readers may like to know that the two wayworn travellers went by train from Jerusalem to Cairo and sailed from Alexandria to Venice, calling at Rhodes and Corfu on the way. From Venice they proceeded to their respective homes at Asolo and in Wales.[1]

90. *To her Father.*

BAALBEK, HOTEL PALMYRA. Saturday, 5.5.28.

DEAREST PIPS,

It seems strange after all this time to be writing from anywhere but Brumana. One feels, when one goes away without thought of return, as if what is left were being shut out of the world; it seems incredible that it all really goes on existing: tea-parties, gossip, heartburnings, politics, and the sunsets beautiful over Beirut as if I were there to see.

[1] In this section the long letters to Mrs. Stark are more of the nature of a diary than most of the letters in the previous sections. It may be worth recording that Freya Stark's books on Southern Arabia owe much of their vividness to their being built up from similar letters to her mother, in which each incident was set down on the day of its occurrence. From many of the letters in the present book purely personal matters have been excised.

We left this morning in a car all to ourselves. We tried to invite the two pleasant young men, and successfully avoided all the elderly ladies who wanted to come, and we had a hot drive down to the valley and up Lebanon through summer green and masses of lavender, cystus, rose, and rhododendron, and then down the bare red side where the hills are folded in strata, and along the flat land between the two ranges: Hermon out of sight, and everything hazy and dusty in the hot sun with the cold air running through it.

And we came here and have a room with the ruins opposite: square blocks, and six immense grand columns against a zebra ridge of snow. We are going to look after tea. One should take one's ruins carefully in small doses between meals.

It is quite different seeing things from a hotel. They become mere objects at once instead of being part of the enchantment. But it is only till Tuesday—for the Adventure is to be after all and we are going among the Druses. Our beds and kitchen, Najm and his small nephew and three donkeys are to meet us Monday morning in Damascus, and we hope to go south into the wilderness on Tuesday morning early and as inconspicuously as possible, in case the French think us dangerous. We have one letter of introduction and a small gun (Najm's) with 100 cartridges, only for quails I trust. We have to buy a water-skin, as the water there is poisonous, and presents instead of money to offer in return for hospitality.

I meant to bring this off all along, but pretended even to myself that I had given up after my illness—with a subconscious feeling, however, that it was just pretence. When Venetia came there was no doubt left. There is a certain madness comes over one at the mere sight of a good map. She had three days' rest, chiefly filled with packing our things in four different lots for various parts of Asia, and in saying good-bye. It was quite sad. Everyone has been so nice to me all through, and putting up with a great many shocks. They don't know our present plan: that will be a parting flutter to leave as a souvenir. Mlle. told me no one had ever done so much stirring up of missionaries in Brumana before.

DAMASCUS. 6.5.28.

We were up early this morning and managed the ruins very well, shaking off guides. We found a sunny corner and sat there to meditate, and to watch the lovely colour of the old stone, tawny and red and black exactly like the hills behind it. There is a wonderful sweep of Lebanon to the north, one immense ridge of melting snow, and a curly dragon of cloud lying round its knees throwing a deep blue shadow; then red country sloping down to where the Baalbek oasis begins—for it is an oasis of trees in the shaven landscape, poplars, fruit and corn, all brilliant green.

There are still the great steps to the temple, by courts and porticos and rows of niches: the steps are cut into huge blocks, six or seven out of one piece of stone. It is not as good as the Acropolis: what can be? Not so *fine*: just the difference between Greece and Rome. But immensity of size is impressive. The guide-book says that three blocks in the west wall are the biggest ever used in architecture: and one *feels* the size too, acting harmoniously like strength. There is one beautiful square door immensely high. The temple inside is nearly perfect too, all but the roof; and there the little hawks were flying with shrill cries and black outlines of feathers clear round their white bodies—or they looked white against the blue. Swallows, and hawks, and lizards, and little far figures of tourists clambering: all small busy lives running among these ruins, which seemed to belong to the land itself rather than to anything human in it: as if the worship of Baal and Helios and Jupiter, and then Theodosius's temple; and then the Moslem walls, were all inherent secrets which had flowered inevitably one after the other in that wilderness of tumbled stones and columns.

We left after lunch against a strong west wind, the plain and hills all colours under the sun and clouds, and came spinning along the solitary Damascus road with nothing in sight. At last we saw two good-sized animals ahead of us, and one tiny donkey, the smallest mite you can think of, trotting along on neat little ankles. When we got nearer, Najm appeared, and the nephew, and our luggage under them, looking Oriental as possible. We waved, much exhilarated. Though how that poor little beast is to trot with the others I don't know, and it'll be I who have to ride him out of mere respect to a sense of proportion.

We met Miss Newton in the hotel at Baalbek. She is a champion of the Arabs and I had an introduction to her. She was most discouraging and said we would certainly be turned back by the French, and advised us to ask responsible opinions. Now that is what I call bad advice. There is an Arab proverb which says: "The wise man sits by the river, but the fool gets across barefoot," and that is what we are going to do. And I think we can tackle a Frenchman.

I feel often as if you were here with me. How I wish I could make you see it all. I am getting to love these huge empty landscapes where you live with the sky as if you were at sea.   Your FREYA.

91. *To her Mother.*

DAMASCUS. 7.5.28.

DARLING B.,

Only a note, for I am so tired after a chaos of a day, and we are off, or hope to be, at six to-morrow morning.

I went shopping all the morning, for food and lanterns and useful things. Then a wearing time after lunch, with Najm, bargaining over saddlebags and presents suitable for Druses. Such a funny mixture : four razors, five pocket-knives, four pieces of white cambric for the gentlemen's heads and the same for the ladies, five mirrors, one pair of scissors, reels of cotton, needles, buttons, and five small rubber balls with landscapes on them for the children; besides a box of Damascus sweets for the chief to whom I have a letter. Najm bargains with a look of innocence. He has nice brown eyes with flecks in them like the skin of a trout, and a good martial moustache. His profile, when his headgear with all its tassels, etc., is on and his rifle slung behind him, is quite fine, except that his figure is skimpy and he wears yellow boots. The rifle is kept among my underclothes at present: I discovered it there when I went to look at things in the khan. What a magnificent feeling it is to go and see one's beasts feeding

in the khan among the sheep and camels and muleteers
and drivers! One needs a microscope to find my donkey,
but there it is—" a poor thing but mine own " for ten days
at least, and with new gilt stirrups. Whether our legs can
stretch to the wooden saddles is a discovery for to-morrow.

I called on my old home. And then on the Bahist
tanner, who was not there but visited me after dinner
together with his son and a gentleman from India (also
dusky). They were sitting in a row in the hotel lounge
as I came out from the dining-room with Dr. Azm (Venetia
had tiresomely collapsed with headache just when she was
wanted as a chaperon). The American tourists stared.
Four Moslems at once and three of them blackish was too
much even for the hotel staff, who are supercilious ever since.

My Sheikh is very happy, for the death sentence on
his brother and brother-in-law is recalled. He wishes
I were to be here to see Damascus turn topsy-turvy over
their return. The elections have brought in a nationalist
majority: they are all full of enthusiasm. The place also
full of troops, more so than when I left.

We came into a large assembly yesterday, banners,
speeches and all in the big square; a holiday, my Sheikh
said, to commemorate the twenty-five men hung by Jemal
Pasha on this day. I was surprised at such a cheerful
commemoration. "It is because they were the first to
die for Syrian freedom," said he.

I must stop. Venetia is longing to go to sleep, and
to-morrow is all before us. We are going to meet our
equipage outside the town so as not to hit the policeman
in the eye. They say the Jebel Druse is closed country.

Your own FREYA.

92. *To her Mother.*

DEIR ALI. 8.5.28.

DEAREST B.,

It looks as if the Adventure were here. Anyway
here are we, settled for the night among the Druses, and
very happy: except that a tragedy has occurred about the
water. We were so anxious to be inconspicuous in Damascus that we left Najm alone with the loading, and he forgot.

He brought along our beasts and luggage to where the tramlines end—a small caravan of three bulging out wider than it was long, with the empty water-skin dancing friskily at the very top of the pyramid. Najm says never mind, and has now got the thing full of a yellow liquid which will suffer no visible change when turned into tea: but we have qualms.

We had to keep for three hours to the high road and had shocks with every policeman. No more than suspicious looks so far, however. The beasts trot along in quite a brisk, though wayward, way: it took them no time to discover we are not experts with the single rein: when they are absent-minded one says "hah" in a bass voice and holds on; their awakening makes the saddle rock like a boat and is particularly sudden if you happen to be sitting sideways: otherwise you ride astride with your legs very far apart and a flat space of saddle in front, useful for resting the map or camera. At present I can hardly sit *anywhere*, after five hours at a stretch and no muscles to do it with. We were to go on another two in the cool of the evening, but one of the Druses has been murmuring that the next village is Circassian and bad, and Najm has settled that we stay here. Delicious feeling! All places are alike to us.

We happened on the only Moslem family in this village. They live in what they call a garden—a beanfield in shadow under old olive trees, full of birds singing: and a small brook flows through in and out of their plots of melons. We have been sleeping in the shade with our heads on the saddlebags while Najm tells as much of our life history as he can invent.

There is wild stony country all around, a hill of shady blackish rock on our left called the Castle of Brass: a Turkish fort, they say, on the top, but now only heaps of stones. The valley strip is green corn: no trees as we came along except one clump round a village very effectively arranged with its flat roofs dark against Hermon in the west. The country was desolate on the whole, for we left the rich land on our right with the main road after passing Kiswe. Pharpar wanders there through poplar groves, a deep green water: you can trace its coil of trees far away among the red hills, where water is indeed "the lives of men!"

It was good going quietly along the main road, watching the country open, chatting to wayfarers, very like life when it is sensible and peaceful. An old roadmender came riding alongside on a white donkey, his blue eyes very northern under a white headdress. He told us of a miraculous well not far away from Katana, where the moon is visible in the water long before she appears in the sky. Then we talked of robbers and Beduins—how two of Najm's party were attacked and killed ten years ago. He pointed to a bridge and told us how he once came upon a shot and dying man lying there. He wanted us to be interested and not alarmed and it was fun to watch him keep the balance. We were glad of a little melodrama, for the landscape was very monotonous. Everything that grows has spikes. The space between us and the Indian Ocean is chiefly covered with small sharp pebbles: a wasteful form of cosmic activity.

Hospitality is a law here; nobody will be paid. The women gathered an apronful of beans for us, and brought leban, and wood for a fire, and Najm cooked rice, and the little girl, Amina (which means faithful) came and talked. Sitting there in the green shadows, with demure little features and pretty manners and the cotton sheet wrapping her body in purple chequered draperies, she might have been Mary playing in her quiet garden. When the news of our coming spread, a circle gathered. The people's manners are perfect—free-born and very friendly. I offered them cigarettes. Najm is a good Druse—strict about these matters and never smokes himself but "when no one is about . . . and to honour the lady"; the other Druses said exactly what my Sheikh said about the wine last night. Your own FREYA.

93. *To her Mother.*

SAWARA EL KEBIR. 9.5.28.

DEAREST B.,

We were just then interrupted by four of the village men of Deir Ali who came upon us where we hoped to have discovered solitude, and left us not another minute of daylight to ourselves. I don't know how we are to get time even to write, for we are *never* alone when in a village: we are now only having a short respite to sleep off our ride.

It has been a fantastic time. The four men came along looking just like the villains in badly-drawn illustrations of seventy years ago and settled down on the ground beside us. One of them informed us he was to be our host for the night. He was dressed in a long blue gown and an ancient black kafiye on his head, which had no top to it. He did not look very reassuring, but actually he has been the most kind and thoughtful host.

The whole party led us to the roof of the house, up a ladder, and a city man from Damascus came to entertain us, being considered more equal to the task, though we liked our country friends infinitely more. We sat through the sunset, watching Hermon and the broad valley, and the herds coming to the brook to drink. The people are grieving, for there has been hardly any rain, and the crops have died and they cannot even make the oxen work for next year, for they have no fodder for them to work on. It is going to be a bad year here on the fringe of the desert. They have no other crop and no other work to turn to. It is quite miserable to go through miles and miles of stubble as if it were already after harvest time.

10.5.28.

After we had sat a long time on the roof, and more men had gathered round us, we were invited down to the court of the house, where two camels and our three donkeys were tied to the enclosing yellow mud wall. There was a low platform against the house, and they had spread us a carpet and a pile of cushions for our elbows, and we sat and watched the pot cooking over a fire indoors, and the women with long white veils wrapped well over the mouth walking to and fro with their beautiful barefoot walk, attending to the supper, carrying little oil lights as the night darkened, and looking like so many Tanagra figures moving noiselessly. It was very wonderful; and quiet: the animals munching peacefully with a little tinkle of bells now and then: two small pomegranate trees in flower over the top of the wall against the western sky.

When it grew quite late and dark we were conducted into a big whitewashed room with a fire in an open fireplace in the corner and carpets spread for us all—six men besides our party. We took off our shoes, and they put a round basket mat before us, and leban, rice, olives, cheese and eggs in little dishes. We were their first European visitors. They gave us spoons, but we preferred to try scooping our dinner up with the bread and caused much pleasure and amusement. It was all beautifully clean—very different from Damascus. The women waited on us. Dogs, cats and children came as near as they dared. Venetia was much cleverer than I at the management of the bread. I was, as a matter of fact, almost giddy with the long ride and the effort of talking Arabic for about five hours after it.

When we had finished, the women ate what was left, and then cleared it all away, while our host made the coffee. He roasted the beans in a shallow scoop and handed them to a young man there who beat them in a mortar with a huge pestle, beating to a cheerful tune: it is an art and needs lots of skill and strength. Venetia had never tasted this excellent drink, and they were all very pleased with our praises. Presently the chief Moslem came in, a fearful old villain to look at, like the Ogre with bloodshot eyes, which were almost worst when he tried to look pleasant. He alone smoked a hubble-bubble; the others took our cigarettes, while we all discussed the harmfulness of smoking in general. The genuine oriental view came from our host, who looked up from where he was crouching over the fire to say that it is God and not the tobacco who sends the diseases; so that I suppose it makes no odds how many bad things you indulge in.

We were very tired. I felt broken to bits, and very glad when they took us out to sleep. There was a murmured consultation as to whether there would be too many bugs for us indoors: "They are not accustomed," said Najm anxiously. I pretended not to listen but was very decidedly in favour of a bed in the open when the suggestion was made. They spread our platform with mattresses and quilts; we looked up into a sky full of white clouds, and pools of stars; and were very happy. When the moon rose I woke up and saw the two camels padding out from

Deir Ali on their way to reach Damascus at dawn. It seemed incredible that this was really I! It was not exactly comfortable: there was a sort of hill under my mattress which began to move in the middle of the night, and turned out to be 'Arif, the small nephew: it must have been worse for him than for me, but after all I had not asked him to settle with all me and my bed on top of him. As for fleas, Keating's has succumbed to numbers.

Your own FREYA.

94. *To her Mother.*

SHAHBA. 11.5.28.

DEAREST B.,

I shall never catch up. Now, however, we have a few hours before us, being virtually prisoners among the French officers who have us here on their hands in the middle of their country, and are anxious to get us out again without hurting our feelings, and yet without letting us see the Druses. But I must tell you all this in order.

We had a good start from Deir Ali. Hot milk to drink, and left at 5.30 in the early light, meeting the village women as they came to the water: very beautiful the grey world in the tender morning and the bright clothes and glittering ornaments of the women—gold coins on their heads under a white veil, just glimmering through. They wear long tight bodices which give a charming grace and slimness to their figures. The bodice is laced with silver ornaments down the front, and the numerous little plaits of their hair are also fastened with silver trinkets under the veil.

The dress itself is very voluminous—long drawers and a skirt over; an apron over this, all dark, and then an overskirt open down the front and richly embroidered with the beautiful designs they still make up out of their own imaginations. Over this they wear another overdress with sleeves, also open and embroidered, and sometimes a bright sash below the waist where the bodice ends. The older matrons do not have the bodice fastened at all but let it support their breasts on either side leaving it open down the middle, which looks very insecure. They are always pleased when we admire their clothes, and are disposed to agree that they are prettier than ours. They are beautiful to see coming up from the water with the lovely movement of the arm upheld to the jar on their shoulder. Alas, we have been seeing them with petrol cans; but at Deir Ali they had the good earthenware pitchers painted with waves and red stripes, like the pre-Homeric potteries.

We left the Hill of Brass and went along between the desert and the sown, or between what was still growing and what had died for want of water, fields and fields of desolate ploughed land hardly recognizable under so many stones. We came by a little bit of rushy grass with water between turfy banks, and there were ponies grazing and it was suddenly Dartmoor. And then we passed Merjana, the first of the basalt villages, and it was black as ink over which dust has been thrown. They are imposing from a way off. When you come near, they are mostly heaps of lava stone.

Najm was very nervous. He told us these were all bad people and Circassians: synonyms to a Druse. We had a few words with one by the wayside, but he did nothing more violent than to invite us to spend the night in his village.

We were travelling across a nearly level plain, with the Brass Hill behind us and the blue of Jebel Druse ahead, with the flats of Hauran on our right and Hermon beyond, and little volcanic tells on our left. The landscape was already dancing and quivering though it was still early. We saw the little tells disappearing in heat: they turned to blue spots raised above the horizon, and then vanished into the white of the sky. In front of Jebel Druse was a speckly flat land still indistinguishable, but getting gradually clearer. We finally saw it to be the low ridge of Leja with Burak standing on its edge like a fortress, quite black.

There was a good military road running through this lonely country. Suddenly we saw a car spinning along it behind us and just as absurd in that place as a car in a movie. It came to a stop beside us, and there were three very agitated French officers inside, who began bawling to ask Najm the way and swearing at their chauffeur all in one breath, and equally uselessly, for neither understood French. I have an idea they thought they were being led astray on purpose. Najm was just like a stodgy cairn terrier with his bristles up. I tried to kick my beast into the scene of action, and managed it with great slowness if not dignity, and asked politely if I could be of any use. You should have seen what a wave of stupefaction went visibly over that motor car; and the man whose language had been so vivid showed that he had still a capacity for blushes. They asked for Burak, and I told them, and they rushed off only too glad to see the last of us without asking questions, and sped away in the *opposite* direction to that they had asked for, which mystery we never cleared.

Najm seemed very reluctant about Burak, but we have long stopped taking advice. As soon as we got into the village, we saw people coming out at us like rabbits from the low doorways. They were the most unattractive crowd you ever saw, all with high cheekbones and slanting eyes, young fellows chiefly, and talking a language of which I could not understand a word. They took us into a large room and set us down on mats and cushions and went on talking among themselves, casting glances at us: they would reply to our poor little remarks in Arabic, and then set to again in their uncomfortable language. After a while we thought we would try to get away and suggested that we should go and see the town; but we were merely told to sit still and rest. We began to be anxious to be well out of it. Najm had that air of angelic meekness which he always puts on when he is in difficulties or with people he dislikes; we also gathered from a few remarks that these people were enemies of the Druses; I realized that they were Circassians, and was rather afraid there might be trouble for Najm if they found out about him. He sat looking as if butter wouldn't melt in his mouth while they told him of Druse murders.

Finally, an elderly woman came in, swathed in black like a nun; she sat herself down beside us and was the only person who seemed human in the room. She told us that they really were Circassians who had come there forty years before (just after Porter's description of Burak as a

deserted city) and had inhabited three villages here ever
since, and how only the younger people speak Arabic as
well as Turkish. An old man now came with lunch on a
tray: he had a beard and rather a nice Mongol appearance;
he was a charming old man in fact. He set the tray down,
with flat bread, leban, cucumber, and omelet, and made
us drink some unattractive water which we swallowed
because we felt it was less dangerous than refusing it; it
was the colour of peat water.

The feeling of the room was still very hostile, all except
the woman and the old man who crouched on his heels beside us flapping away the flies with a towel, which was kind
but made eating difficult. I suddenly had a happy thought:
I took up the leban and said: "Yoghourt"; it just shews
the use of language! The word acted like magic and
everybody smiled. After that we had no more uneasiness.
We went round the ruined streets, heaps of black stones
with houses here and there, seventeen centuries old and
many still intact, with roofs of solid stone slabs and windows and doors too, solid sheets of black stone turning in
stone sockets. I measured one door and found it a span
in thickness, and tried hard to move it but couldn't, but
the people there swing them to and fro. We finally parted
from them all on the edge of Leja amid blessings, and one
young man came down to show us the Roman cistern in
the plain, a huge square tank with steps leading down to it,
the water looking rather sinister reflecting the black stone.
I hope all our photos will come out.

By this time it was about eleven and everything swimming in heat, and nothing but the fear that these people
might discover about Najm made us go on along by the
edge of Leja, which drops from a low ridge of dismal rubble
on to an equally dismal stony plain. We tried to induce
Najm to let us rest in the shade of an old square fort which
stood on our left from the village, but he had had as much
as he could bear and refused, saying that it was no rest to
keep a look-out for Beduins. We didn't point out that it
was he and not we who would have to do the looking out,
but went on meekly in a sort of coma, even meditation
drowned in the sun which seemed to be cooking us like

pancakes as it was refracted from the lava slabs. Our poor
little donkeys went with their heads down, and slipping on
the stone. I realized for the first time that one has to
clothe oneself against the heat. An old Haurani man
caught us up here, trotting barefoot over the blazing
ground, and it was pleasant to see his gentle face after all
those high cheekbones, and he was useful, too, as a guide,
for the track was nearly invisible till we reached the
"Sultan's Way" again, which wanders in sandy loneliness
round Leja's outer edge.

Just on the corner where Leja and the road turn south
there is Sawara el Kebir, another good black outline of a
village. We meant to rest there till evening and then go
on, but we found such a charming welcome and were
begged to stay, and were put to rest in a cool room in a fine
big house after a drink of leban, and above all we were left
alone: so that we felt this was simply a taste of heaven, and
why move? Six hours is quite a lot on a donkey. We lay
on deliciously soft mattresses through the afternoon. The
father of the family must have died; anyway, he was not
en evidence and the place seemed well under the thumb of
its women, who ran it very competently: there was the
mother, rather meek, and a buxom aunt who ruled the
whole establishment, and Nur, aged seventeen and the
loveliest thing to look at in the world. The men were
comparatively quite unimportant, and though a marriage
was later suggested to me with the son of the house, that
was aunt's doing also and I believe he was not even
consulted. He would have been a shock to you as a son-
in-law, though his eyebrows were really very fine, slanting
towards each other with the slight perfect curve of two
bows over his eyes, which were of course blackened with a
pencil line below them. This slant of the eyebrow seems
very characteristic of the Beduin Arab.

We went with Nur to the water-fetching after the sun
had gone, and saw the same doors and windows as at
Burak, and a good old temple door and a pillared room:
there is no reason, except in the destructiveness of men,
why this building should not last like the pyramids, for
there is nothing about it that is not stone.

The water-tank was like Burak, but a gentler scene, for

all the village was gathered in friendly leisure. There
was a goatherd filling the trough for about a hundred black
goats to drink in turn: he was a half-naked Beduin, as wild
and skinny as some Goya John the Baptist, standing against
the skyline drawing up the cans of water. The women
stood about waiting, chatting, Christians and Druses in a
friendly way—for they share this village. We had met
one of the Christians already at the house, tattooed and
dressed in blue like a Beduin and sitting on the floor with
a sewing machine. Now we saw that they all wore the
same costume: in times of massacre it must mean that
St. Bartholomew is already prepared on both sides.
Venetia sat and sketched, but found it hard with so many
enthusiasts round her: whether it was a goat or a baby,
they would push the creature almost on to her paper and
expect a portrait. She managed one quite creditable
infant, and pleased the parent, who took the picture away
after making her draw a hand with five outspread fingers
underneath it as a talisman.

The youngest son of the house came strolling back with
us, talking appalling French to V. He asked me to
embrace him as a brother: we are getting tactful in these
predicaments; I told him I would treat him as an English
brother and shake his hand.

At the house we found that the schoolmaster had come
to call on us. He had a fine, delicate face, and talked bad
French taught by the Jesuits; and told us that frequent
tourists came to Sawara, a statement which we doubted
at the time and which our military friends have now
decidedly contradicted.

Najm had been shooting larks all day. He is a particularly bad shot, but the creatures are so tame, they sit
on stones and hop about these barren lands without fear.
We were always glad when Najm missed them, but could
not help finding them very good for dinner.

After dinner visitors began to drop in. Various wild-
looking cousins with the same tilted eyebrows and long
hair and blackened eyes. More and more came—all men
of course; but these people's manners are truly *good*: the
aunt came to sit beside us so that we should not feel uncomfortable; and Nur hovered at the window and at last crept

in and sat by her aunt also, her white veil well arranged over her mouth and chin: and one could see that her aunt had not the heart to scold her away.

My Arabic goes completely mad when I am tired: it was a great strain to be chief visitors in a circle of over twenty strangers after such a long day. The eldest son brought the rebeck in and we had music, very skilfully played on his one string, wayward and mournful as wind. Then Najm began to sing with 'Arif, who is a sturdy little boy of thirteen with a good voice and a snub nose and a round mouth, and will walk along for hours in silence till he breaks into some sudden confidence. And then three men got up and danced the Dabki, all holding hands and going through different formal steps. I noticed what an important thing the bare foot is in a dance, and what art in just a subtle placing of the heel or little twist of a muscle; it becomes as expressive as the hand can be. There was a gay scamp of an old sheikh who was great at the Dabki: his eyes gleamed out under his bushy eyebrows and he twisted his old body from side to side in the most daredevil way.

They were very friendly and took much trouble over us. I happened to say that I liked the music of the pipes, and they sent at once for the expert who played them—a handsome creature with two long pigtails falling over his hands as he sat on the floor holding the double reeds to his lips. It was a curious gathering in the flickering light. Most of the men had European coats—military loot many of them, with the regiments still shewing on the buttons. They wore their long gowns under, and the Beduin white draped head-dress held in place with the black camel-hair cord. The older sheikhs always keep to the true Druse head-dress, however, and that is a very neat white turban, quite small and wound tightly, like a skull cap.

They all left us at last, and the women came in and then they began to talk. The unfortunate guest has double labour when host and hostess have to be spoken to separately. It was a great affair to settle whether or not we were to sleep alone: they made up their minds finally that only the aunt and the son of the house should sleep with us: on what principle the selection was made we could not discover. Under the circumstances it would, we felt, be indelicate to admit to undressing; but Venetia ventured to put her pyjamas on over her clothes and this had a great success, and she was taken into the family bedroom next door and examined with shouts of laughter: though, as we pointed out to the ladies, they themselves wear very much the same sort of objects by day as well as by night.

The aunt as a matter of fact looked well in *déshabille* with two long black plaits coming down when her veil was off, and the gold coins, in which she sleeps, shining like a crown. She also kept on a silver amulet slung like a bandolier over her white petticoat. Nur's hair was differently done, in numerous tiny plaits all weighted with red silk cords ending in silver tassels: she told me the name, but I have forgotten, and she said that the weight was good for the head. The hairdressing has to be done once a month. One of the little plaits is neatly arranged to come under the chin so that they can tuck the veil into it. I had been puzzling as to how they managed to hold it up over the mouth. Nur was very anxious to sleep beside me with her arms round my neck, but this excess of affection was discouraged, to my relief. When we were all tucked in, the son of the house came to his bed in the corner: but he was troubled, because V. and I, instead of sleeping, went on murmuring to each other about things like Keating's, and so the poor man crept out again to sleep on the balcony, and the aunt came and explained the matter. If this is not true thoughtfulness, what is? We accepted the sacrifice gratefully. WE didn't sleep till after twelve, for there were a great many fleas: I suppose one may get accustomed. Whenever I woke in the night I heard V. pumping at that little sprayer.

That is all I have to tell you about Sawara. Here at Shahba we have just been interrupted by a conversation through the partition of our bedroom (every word comes through, and it is a great cramp to V.'s and my conversation). It is the Intelligence Officer and one of his native police, and he is telling him that we are to be allowed about so long as we shew no sign of wishing to pry into the affairs of their tiresome war; otherwise we are to be taken to the nearest officer (rather guesswork this for it's all in Arabic). I suppose we are intended to hear as it is being said so loudly. We don't want to enquire about their war; in fact we want to get away from it and them at present. But if I were as nervous as all that I should take jolly good care to hide it more.

Your own FREYA.

95. *To her Mother.*

SHAHBA.   11.5.28.

DARLING B.,

When we left Sawara at five on Thursday morning we thought we were to have a grey day for a change. We followed the high road—the Sultan's Way—and found that it took us through flat corn country with Leja just out of sight on our right and only the black villages appearing on its edge. That is how, quite accidentally but providentially, we missed falling into the hands of the garrison at Khul Khuly—where we had meant to sleep the night before and whence we would probably have been sent back from the Jebel Druse altogether. We passed it in the distance, saw the French flag waving on its guardhouse, and then, finding the main road dull, turned over ploughed land and discovered a mule-track leading from village to village close by the Wadi Liwa which looks like a snaky moat round the fortress of Leja and can be traced by its clumps of green shrub, though there is no water in it.

V. was feeling sick and faint that morning. We went on for some time, then she thought milk and a rest would be the thing, so we turned aside and found a well of the usual dirty water, with a dead sparrow floating in it, and decided to picnic. There was no shade, there is not a tree in all this country; but the sky was cloudy. We sent 'Arif for the milk, and were just beginning to enjoy tea over the spirit lamp and the bliss of being alone, when he returned with the villagers, and we were slowly but quite irresistibly forced to accept hospitality. Killed with kindness, we are being.

Redeme is the village, and it is divided into two parts,

and a stony bit between them, and one is Druse and the other Christian. The latter got at us first; a simple peasant man, very anxious to make us happy. The Druses dropped us as soon as they saw us with their enemies, for they are still at daggers drawn in Redeme. They fraternised with Najm and his gun at a distance. We were left in the hands of a horrid little worm of a school-master who first tried to induce us to throw over our peasant host and go to him, and then began lamenting that we—Christian ladies—should let ourselves be taken about by a Druse guide. Venetia considers me weak in the matter of snubbing, but I did my best on this occasion; I did so dislike him, and his French was villainous: but he was insuppressible. How one loathes these products of European education when one sees them next to the genuine article of the country!

We insisted on going to our peasant's house, and found his living-room vaulted with the ancient stone, washed a deep ochre; the floor of solidified dung and a huge porous water jar catching the light from the door. His handsome wife, dressed in Beduin blue as at Sawara, received us, and cooked the birds while the men started the coffee at the central hearth.

These Christians spoke a barbarous sort of Arabic, pronouncing k as ch, and q like g; it was quite incom-prehensible to me. They were a very handsome lot, unvisited by the world, and rougher than at Sawara: we were the first Europeans ever known to have stayed there, except for the French when they opened the school. The groups gathered in the shaft of light from the door; they looked amazingly picturesque against that yellow back-ground; the *violence* of the beauty here is so surprising: it springs out of ugliness with no transition, like Minerva fully armed, and leaves one breathless.

Our host and hostess were very anxious to do well with their unaccustomed visitors, and troubled because we would eat nothing more substantial than our birds, which we tore to bits with our teeth in front of the interested audience quite calmly, Venetia reviving visibly as the process went on. They all thought her in the last stages of disease; I had to assure them very seriously that it was

L

not consumption. There are no doctors in these villages: "Either we are well or we die," said our host. His little daughter was ill, with a heart thumping terribly and I did what I could, telling them to let her lie flat and keep her going with coffee and take her as soon as they could to Tell Khaldiye where there is a M.O. for the garrison. Our unspeakable schoolmaster assured us that this man would not attend to a civilian patient: at the time I thought this merely a reflection of the little bounder's own brutality, but now that we have got to know the army of occupation more intimately—why, I should not wonder if it were true.

We had explained carefully to Najm that we *must* be alone for an hour or so every day: accordingly, after our meal they spread us out one on each side of the coffee hearth to sleep and the audience was scattered; but it went on coming in a continual stream to the doorway to look in, so that we didn't get a very good rest, and about two o'clock we felt we might just as well move on. There is very little to see in Redeme except the big cistern of rain-water as in all the other villages, and the lower story of an old tower which they told us had been much damaged during the fighting two years ago. I imagined the Druse half of the village walked across the dividing space and played havoc with our friends: the feeling is still high anyway, and when we went to visit the Druse Sheikh the Christians did not accompany us but stood gathered on the edge of the dividing space to watch us very much as a flock of sheep might do if two of their number suddenly decided to pay an afternoon call on the wolves.

The wolves were extremely pleased and Najm simply swelling with satisfaction as he showed us off to his friends. We realized that we should have offended seriously by omitting this ceremony. The Druses really have much better manners. I am not sure that the fact of keeping the women as such absolute inferiors does not help to give the men their remarkable dignity: even the poorest always has someone in his own house on whom to practise the manners of a king, and so the grand air comes natural. I am not saying the game is worth the candle, but the manner is certainly there and very pleasant to find. The Druses have only one wife, and if they divorce her they

can never change their minds and marry her again, as the
Moslems may do.

We felt we must pacify the Christian part of the village
by visiting the school, and found a charming picture—
about thirty little figures in long gowns to their feet and
bright round caps learning their lessons in rows in a small
building with a French flag floating from the window.

Then we left Redeme, after presenting our Druse host
with a pocket-knife: I have to be rather careful about
presents; Najm hates to see the goods of this world falling
into the hands of infidels: the poor Circassians got nothing
at all out of him.

We followed along the Leja track. This is wild country,
full of ruined stones and cities, a sad beauty of its own over
its greyness. Here you reckon time from Sunrise to Sunset.
You greet hastily on the road to see if it is to be Peace, if
your greeting is returned. Life has the charm of being
secured at a cost of personal endeavour, a thing sweet
because not valued too highly. That surely is freedom.

There was a grey sky, and an arid hot wind from the
west. We came by a lonely waterhole; three riders were
there talking to sitters by the well, the long tails of the
horses and the leader's bright green cloak swishing about
in the wind. They kindly wheeled about to let me take a
picture. The man in green was the Sheikh of Imtune,
the next village: he went off like a centaur, his beautiful
little Arab picking its way among the stones.

Regaining the Sultan's Way we turned south-west
as the afternoon wore on. We had left Redeme at 2.45.
Imtune on our right looked a miserable sort of place for
the night, and we decided to push on to Shahba even after
dark, though Najm disliked the idea of night on the road.
The country became a little gentler, pale yellow or green
where the corn was not too dead, and swelling into round
tells with a feeling of England about their sudden grassy
sweeps in the evening light. It is marvellous what a
variety of things the sky can do with a treeless landscape.

Our road led up towards the hills, the same that had
looked so blue from Deir Ali. We left Tell Shibhan,
a pudding shape, on our right, padded through a belt of

black coal-dust, and saw Shahba in the dusk, almost
indistinguishable among the black stones of its hillside,
and spread along the ridge. The light was failing. Little
white dianthus flowers, a kind I have never seen and
smelling sweet like jasmine, were just visible by the roadside:
the people were bringing in the last loads of their harvest.

Our poor donkeys stumbled about, very tired; we had
done seven and a half hours that day. Just before it got
quite dark we clattered through the Roman gate, half
ruined, and found a broad Roman street, its houses in
heaps on either hand. Our hoofs rang on the pavement:
it was as if we entered among ghosts. We came to where
the triumphal arch once stood, at the crossing of two
great streets, and went uphill, past three temple columns.
White-turbaned Druses were sitting at the doorsteps. It
was as if all the centuries were whispering behind them.
We knocked at the door we had been told of, and the
women welcomed us, and made us rest in a charming
yellow room—always the same ochre wash—decorated
with paintings and the bright round mats all hung along
the walls. And we let ourselves fall into sheepskin rugs,
took our shoes off, washed our hands and faces, and were
just sinking into perfect contentment when the French
military got us.

Your own FREYA.

96. *To her Mother.*

SHAHBA. 11.5.28.

DARLING B.,

I left off just at the interesting moment when two
men in khaki—native police—came in to say that their
officer would like us to visit him. We really are still
remarkably innocent. We took it for a message of kindness,
and thought we would pay a call before supper and get it
over. Our men led us along, through a whole boxful of
matches, up and down stairs without railings where one
seemed about to fall off the edge every minute. Venetia
was just turning into a black doorway, when they told her
it was the prison: which was an omen, no doubt. At last
we climbed on to a little square terrace in the light of a

petroleum lamp and found six astonished French officers—
really extremely astonished. They had thought our
arrival, when it was announced to them, a hallucination of
their police, and were in the midst of dinner. I don't think
I have ever seen people so completely nonplussed before.

We murmured politely and were going to retire, but
this woke them up and a young man in white uniform
made it evident that he was the head, and that we were not
to go our own ways any longer. We were not to go back
to our hosts, not even to see about luggage, certainly not
to speak to them: we were not to speak to Najm by ourselves. But he was sent for and the wretched Mustashar—
which means one of whom advice is asked and is what the
Intelligence Officers are called here—told him in what we
thought a very arrogant manner that the people of the
house were not to trouble about us any more, or words to
that effect; our luggage was to be kept at the *poste*.

I had a qualm thinking of my little book, where I had
written disrespectfully of their colonial government and
which they would find if they searched. Najm wore the
same expression of non-committal innocence which he puts
on for the Circassians: he just turned his head from the
Mustashar's Arabic and looked to see if I meant to confirm
it. I had a second's hesitation whether to let on about
knowing the language or not, as I knew it would make our
case worse, but it was the only way of communicating
with Najm. I was also getting red in the face with annoyance at hearing him spoken to in that way: so said that he
was to tell our hosts that the Mustashar had "commanded"
us to stay and must be obeyed, and left the six officers none
too pleased, I rather think, with this way of putting it.
They listened in the most freezing silence.

We felt that as we had no choice about remaining, it
was better to do so as guests, and have been very careful to
keep the matter on this footing, which is making it much
more difficult for our poor jailors to do anything about us.
Whatever they suggest in the way of detainment, we thank
them for effusively, and tell them how charming it is to
find such unexpected hospitality, how delightful to have a
bed with nothing in it besides, and water to wash in, with

a policeman to bring it to you. The feminine element
has obviously not been known in Shahba before; the
garrison is straining itself to provide for its comfort. They
have had to turn out of a nice room hung with rugs and
provided with French novels: and they have had to lend
me pyjamas, as they won't let me go to my luggage. Blue
flannelette with a sea-green pattern! Venetia has been
riding in the Intelligence Officer's breeches, which dangle
loosely round her legs. Her blue eyes are almost too much
for the Mustashar. As for me and my Arabic—we are
damned. He is quite sure that I am here to stir up the
Druses, with her as an innocent foil, and he has put us in
this room, which has nothing but thin wood to separate it
from his office. So far he can have heard nothing but
gurgles of laughter, which must be irritating.

It was a comic meal last night. They thought they
were "making us talk," which was fun. Venetia and I
got a minute to ourselves before, as they couldn't refuse us
a chance to powder our noses, and hastily laid down the
plan of defence. They couldn't be expected to believe
that we were wandering merely for pleasure, so we decided
to lay all the blame on Cook's guide-book which (happily)
never mentions the existence of motor roads in the Jebel
Druse. "You should get it brought up to date," said we
reasonably. "It is very *pénible* to go about on donkeys,
and you would have *lots* of tourists if they only knew what
an *easy* country it is." The landscape here is almost
entirely composed of black stones. We could see doubt in
the eyes of the garrison. One young man finally said
that he never thought the *Agence Cook* would be sending
tourists here: we had to explain that we had not been
exactly *sent*. They were in difficulties anyway, for they
were anxious to assure us that the country is in perfect
peace and good order, so they could not harp on our
carelessness of danger. "What danger?" say we promptly.
"Is it not all quiet now?" "Perfectly quiet, Mesde-
moiselles," "We knew that it was quite safe since you
have taken it over," said we, intending to annoy. It does
really rouse one's worst feelings to be taken for a spy, and
the Mustashar was the only gentleman among them.

I had a smug little doctor beside me whose insinuations were a great strain. "No doubt you are interested," said he, "other compatriots of yours travelled here . . . just before the Rebellion." The nice old Commandant with a gentle face and white moustache was the only one who really liked us and would have been glad to talk of less explosive things than Druses. But we were there to answer questions, and did it with a simple truthfulness (all except the matter of Cook's) which astonished them more and more. It seems we have come 89 kilometres across that stony waste: and that English travellers have not come to Shahba since the war: and when we said we had been sleeping in the villages they just looked at each other. They seemed to think it was our fault that the police did not discover us; we refrained from pointing out that it was their business, not ours. But we did say we had come in contact with the Army near Burak, only had found it preoccupied, and in fact that it had seemed rather *ébahi* when we spoke to it. The story had a charming effect at the dinner table, and we felt we were getting our own back. We managed to skim over these abysses on a light level of conversation really quite creditable. Before retiring the Mustashar said very peremptorily that we could not possibly leave on the morrow. We told him we should be delighted to stay, and how kind we thought him, and would he take us out riding? He was quite meek about it, and we have had a gorgeous morning in the hills, and such a pleasant change from donkeys.

Your own FREYA.

97. *To her Mother*.

SHAHBA. 11.5.28.

DARLING B.,

Another scrap of time to tell you about this morning. It was really a pleasant time—at least it would be so if it were not for the disagreeable feeling of being on the wrong side—all black looks or subservience as the case may be, but none of the charming friendliness of before. We should not notice it if it were not for the difference of their treatment before. And the French manners to the natives are really bad, horrid. In everything else our Intelligence Officer is very pleasant, he is taking a lot of trouble about us; and a handsome young man too, which is one of the things in this world of which he is most perfectly persuaded. He has a white uniform which sits very well and gives him a nice slim figure, so that when one looks at Venetia in his breeches it seems remarkable that the same garment can look so tight on one person and so loose on the other.

I doubt if he can understand our lighthearted indifference to all the interference with our plans; we shall see what happens to-morrow when we try to leave. One thing is quite certain: I am not going to let this be turned into a French Conducted Tour. Our bed was not such an oasis of comfort either: we seemed to be sliding off the edge all night and longed for the safety of the Druse floor, and our native police attendant seemed to think he could clean our shoes in one corner while we washed in the other, which I suppose is what is done in barracks; and when we had got rid of him and V. was just trying on the breeches, Najm poked his head through the broken pane of the door with such a pathetic smile that it seemed inhuman to tell him we didn't want to see him while we were dressing.

We finally got out and found six mounted police with carbines and pistols holding our Arab ponies ready saddled; peaked saddles with embroidered flaps and long tassels and a single bright-coloured woollen rein. The police wear khaki, set off with an enormous red kafiye which they swathe round their heads, and clap the black chaplet on top, which is enough to make one forget any ordinary ideas one may have had about a policeman's appearance. We trotted out amid salutes fired into the air: guns slung over the shoulder, belts full of cartridges: the Druses looked at us from their doorsteps. Delicious to be on something that does not jig along with tiny donkey steps. I found the native saddle comfortable enough and no difficulty with one rein.

We clattered out by the straight Roman street with shattered houses, all ruined stones, on either hand; by the ancient baths, through the great ruined gate, up a stony valley, heaped up with ruined volcanic rocks, and green wheat growing in red earth where the water can feed it. The country is all hills, very like the grass and stones of Dartmoor when there is no heather. Old black villages and little towns lying along the crests, and Leja just a greyness in the flat below us, with Shahba spread between two volcanic cones in the foreground, and the Hills of Brass already lost far away in haze.

It was grey and quite cold. The bodyguard rushed round, galloping their ponies in circles, yelling a wild war song of four words over and over, chasing each other with brandished weapons and flying tassels.

We went up to where our lieutenant is building the new reservoir for Shahba, a square thing in cement at the valley head. The people have to give their labour for nothing: and as it is the country people who are made to build it for the convenience of the town I suppose they are not very enthusiastic in the work. It seems to me also that a large store of water must make a difference to the little underground streams that used to trickle below and keep this valley green, and that it may make all below the reservoir less fertile, but I do not know about these things. Anyway it was a pleasure to see clear flowing water: "sweet" is the adjective the Arabs use for the sound of it, and that is what it is when you have been long out of its hearing.

On the top of the round tell at the valley head is a little shrine dedicated to Jesus; it is called Tell el Massieh, the hill of the Messiah, and we climbed our ponies to the top, and a red carpet was spread against the domed roof of the little sanctuary, and we sat there looking over half the world to the desert stretching out in broad and gentle lines, a lovely light upon its solitudes. The white bearded guardian came in his blue jacket, his eyes darkly pencilled, and stood before us where we reclined, and told us the legend: how Jesus slept here, and a little shrine was built, and then Mohammed came and it was forgotten, until the Druses restored it to honour and gave it its name. And then he pointed to the Hill of St. John, and then to the Hill of Khalid ibn el Walid, who buried his child there, so they say; he was one of the great generals of the world, who turned the mill-wheels of Jalula with the blood of his enemies and was nicknamed Sword of God, and I should have liked to talk about him to the old man and would have made him very friendly at once, but I am rather carefully keeping my Arabic as dark as I can. I am already quite an ominous enigma in the Lieutenant's eyes, and V. says that the Interpreter has been murmuring in his master's ears that my Arabic is good. It was tiresome to have to go about being so dignified and not really polite: we were not even allowed to take off our shoes when we entered the shrine, and stood there quite unnecessarily polluting its holiness while the two police, who had followed us in, kissed the empty semblance of a tomb which stood in the middle of the little carpeted room. They kissed it in eight different places, at each corner. It is a great place of pilgrimage and the old man told us that the sacrifices, kids or lambs, are still brought.

We came down the hill shoulder to a Beduin camp. The police drew the tribe up in a line to meet us, and we were taken to the Sheikh's tent and sat at the back behind the coffee-pots in the place of honour, with our arms resting against a camel-saddle. The tribe sat round and gave us coffee and sherbet and a hot drink flavoured strongly with cinnamon—very good: if I had been alone I should have found out how it was made, but we had to be dignified and just sit, and say a word now and then through the interpreter, though the Lieutenant speaks quite adequate Arabic: he says he uses the interpreter so that he may have time to think out his answer, but I can't help feeling that what he gains in dignity is more than lost by want of the cordiality which this system causes.

After a while all the men stood up for a dance. They called a handsome Beduin maid from the women's side of the tent, and dressed her in one of the men's great cloaks and stood in a close row behind her clapping their hands with the long waving white sleeves and giving short low growls, very staccato and incredibly fierce, while the girl sailed up and down in front of them with a little stick in one hand and a handkerchief in the other, the clumsy garment billowing out like a sail, the movements slow and graceful: and the men all bent towards her, the whole line swaying this way and that as she moved, the clapping and growling keeping time together but growing faster and sharper, and faster and sharper, their wild faces half hidden under the dark kafiyes, the eyes shining out and the long dirty sleeves dancing like streamers. It was a marvellous sight.

Your own FREYA.

98. *To her Mother.*

SHAHBA. 12.5.28.

DARLING B.,

Yesterday was outstanding even in our crowded history.

After finishing our letters we went about the town with Najm, who is in depths of gloom and apparently suffering from a regular inquisition from the police. I got him alone for a few seconds and just had time to explain to him what idiots they are, when two accompanying shadows joined us, very kindly, to shew us the sights of Shahba. I was rather pleased in the morning, by the way, for I managed to get at my luggage (with the excuse of pyjamas) and to convey the compromising book into Najm's waist-band under the very nose of a sentry—to Najm's alarm and discomfort.

Shahba has a fine impress of Roman spaciousness about it, though only the skeleton of its glory remains: baths and theatre and three temple columns and a charming temple front that is now the school; but the best of it are the four great streets, twelve metres is the width where the low houses have not encroached; they are spread like a cross down the slope of the hill and end in the ruined gates, and the old pavement is still there. The Mustashar is having the main street rebuilt with shops and doing his best by keeping to the one-storied house of the country, but he is covering up the edges of the pavement and we are trying to point out this barbarism without hurting his feelings. It was fun teasing our police. We wanted to take photos of Druse women, but of course when they saw us not only with men but with policemen, they fled even before we got near them: I devoted my best Arabic to explaining to our escort how much more friendly we found the people when we went about alone.

Late in the day our Lieutenant procured a car and we were sent for to be taken to one of the central villages of Leja, which is the most inaccessible part of the Jebel, the part where hitherto no law ever reached. They have just finished a road through, a few days ago: I must say the French are doing good work in the way of roads. Each village is made to do its own piece under the responsibility of the Mudir or headman. This Mudir came with us: we were going to his house to arrange a wedding which had been rather precipitated; the bridegroom, one of our Lieutenant's police, had carried off the bride without asking anyone's leave, and the matter now had to be arranged. It was rather wonderful climbing up on to that dead plateau in the dusk. The road is cut through the solidified lava which tosses round in craters and crumbling ruins of crags and pinnacles, a hopeless waste land. The second book of *Paradise Lost* describes it. Nothing grows there: but there are old watch-towers and villages, sunken back into the stone chaos, and in the greyness and incredible confusion of that dead land you could not tell which ruins were made by nature and which by man. We crossed this belt by Umm Zeitun (the Mother of Olives, though such a tree does not exist in the country) and reached the cultivated part in the centre of Leja when night had fallen. The car had to jolt slowly over the bumps of the road, and just before we reached the village our armed escort passed us at a wild gallop yelling their war song: *Hoto yoto hozo yozo*— they repeat the four syllables over and over.

The village had turned out to meet us with two big lanterns, and V. and I led the procession swathed in our long Arab cloaks and with a strange feeling that we were walking in a dream. The lanterns were hung on stands near the centre of a high room built, roof and all, of stone slabs, and spanned with two great arches, all washed with yellow ochre. It was the original building of seventeen centuries ago. In the centre were the red embers and a row of coffee-pots with the long beaks shining brightly: and round the four sides crimson carpets were spread, with cushions piled here and there, making a rich harmony with the yellow walls. The wild figures trooped in: village youths with long locks—sometimes as many as ten pigtails, sometimes just a shock of curls over either ear: Druse priests in black gowns and close white turban with a black drapery over the back of it: the soldiery with their cartridge-belts and red head-gear: and the Mudir himself, more or less European, his feet surprisingly clad in pumps. They were intelligent faces with free straight looks: not the perfection of the Beduin manner, but there is something very pleasing especially in the feeling of independence and perfect equality which is almost universal among them; when it is missing, which only happens where the Europeans have spoilt them, one feels what an immense loss it is.

We sat in the place of honour on one side of the hearth; and the Lieutenant, with the Mudir, on the other. We had the view of him reclining like a Roman emperor, in his white uniform with a red ribbon on his breast, running amber beads negligently through his fingers while the Mudir talked to him with great eagerness in a low voice and little groups sat murmuring in the flickering light. The servants were busy with the coffee. The Interpreter, also in white, sat near us, I believe with a vague idea that we required to be reassured. In the middle of the room, looking very anxious, stood the bridegroom whose fate was being decided, the wildest figure for a husband you can imagine with his black curls coming out in shocks under his red kafiye and his khaki overcoat looking as much like an Arab gown as such a garment can be made to look. This went on for a long time. At last a sort of atmosphere of conclusiveness came over the room: the feud I suppose had been settled: the bridegroom came up rather shyly: he was asking the Interpreter whether we should like the wedding before or after dinner. We thought the sooner the better, and that is what the Interpreter said for us.

Neither the bride nor groom appears on these occasions: the young Lochinvar retired, and two representatives sat down crosslegged opposite each other in the empty space behind the coffee-pots, two priests standing at their shoulders. A bracelet and a green kerchief were brought: the two held out their thumbs, upwards, one close to the other, and the bracelet was put over them, joining them together, and the green cloth was then put over that so as to cover the two hands. We were then asked to remain a minute or so in silence and to pray for the young couple, holding our palms outspread on our laps with the thumbs turned outward. The green kerchief was then taken off and the marriage legally over except for the bringing away of the bride, which was to happen later. A great tray of wine and sweets was then brought in, the particular offering of the bridegroom: it was vermouth, the only wine we have yet seen among the Druses. As soon as we had done honour to it, we moved up to our real dinner, two small roasted sheep and little messes of rice: luckily V. had remembered to suggest eggs in time, and I was treated as an invalid and watched with a free mind while the Interpreter dipped his hand neatly into the sheep and heaped Venetia's plate.

I don't really like eating with a roomful of people looking on in a silent circle. When we had done (the Lieutenant of course ate with us) the second lot of guests started: and after them the servants: and that was the end of the sheep. We meanwhile went and sat outside on the long seat by the door while the young men of the village drew themselves up in a line to dance before us—a long semicircle rather— with the lantern on the ground throwing its light up at them, and one youth whose hand-clapping led the chorus: his head-dress had come off and his head was shaven half-way up with about a dozen little plaits dangling all round, and he led very skilfully, singing one verse of a long long chant—a marriage song, I think. The clapping hands all kept time, and the whole gathering took up the refrain, eight syllables, always the same: at intervals they would break off into the dance we had seen among the Beduins, only far wilder, for it was now one or other of the men who would leave his place and come into the middle of the circle, and stand there jerking his body like an epileptic with little rigid jerks all up and down the line, facing the others and clapping furiously, and rousing those opposite him to a perfect frenzy of clapping and growling; then he would dash at one of them and tear off his head-dress, and this man would come into the middle while the other went back into the swaying clapping line; the growls were scarce human; it was like some primitive rage inexpressible in words. The jumping figure in front was indescribably evil, the long gown and flying hair, and frenzy of passion, bent nearly double to urge the others on. The growling and clapping grew faster and faster; the line swayed as one man; the light flickered over them against the blackness of the night; one could not watch without a sort of terror, as if something unknown and appalling were suddenly finding its voice. When it all stopped, the people were quite exhausted.

The Mudir was very anxious that we should go on to drink champagne (of all things) at his own house in the next village. But when we got into the car it appeared that we should have scarce enough petrol to carry us home; suggestions were made that we should try and run it on petroleum; we had a sudden quite unfounded suspicion that the French Intelligence had decided to decoy us on to Leja for the night while they dealt with Najm and our luggage separately. The Lieutenant, however, was quite firm and we said good-bye. Just as we were preparing to go there was a stir: the gathering opened out to make way for a handsome middle-aged man with blue eyes and straight black brows who walked up with quick step and flowing dark draperies; he was the uncle of the abducted bride, and had been absent at the feast and reconciliation. I think he would have liked to remain absent too. He was making the best of a bad business: his coming evidently caused a sensation and much pleasure to the Mudir, who tried to cover up his kinsman's reserved manner by extreme heartiness of his own. The Lieutenant made a condescending speech with a rather sinister ending: "You and I know each other, Muhammed Ali." Muhammed Ali looked as if this fact were true but did not give him pleasure. He did not smile but looked very straight before him. We came away wondering what the drama is. It was nearly eleven and dark, and as we bumped along the new road we had to slow down for hares, who could not understand headlights in their black country and ran stupidly in front of us, unable to escape the strange monster.

Your own FREYA.

99. *To her Mother.*

SULEIME.   13.5.28.

DARLING B.,

    We have got away at last, at six this morning, after friendly farewells.   I was tired yesterday and stayed indoors, quite glad to be in jail.   The garrison was getting fond of us I believe, especially the servants; as for the police, they looked on us as their especial pets.   Last night in the starlight, just when the poor Lieutenant would have liked to say tender farewells to Venetia, I told him how awfully amusing we had found it to be taken for spies; we should have such fun telling it to our mothers when we got home.   The poor man was rather upset.   "How can you think such things, Mesdemoiselles?" says he in a very unnatural voice.   How can we not, with a policeman springing up whenever we put our nose out of doors and poor Najm nearly frantic with cross-questionings!   The Lieutenant, however, had an inkling that we were taking him rather as a joke, and I think he will be glad enough to let us go wherever we like so long as it is out of his particular district.   He made a last effort to make us relinquish donkeys and let ourselves be taken round by a government car.

    We were as tactful as could be; I asked him to tell us what Druses to stay with, and he has given us a letter to the High Priest at Kanawat, and to the Interpreter's father at Salhad.   Then I told him about my letter of introduction to the rebel Mut'ib Bey at Resas; he looked taken aback, at my frankness I believe, for he had found out about the matter independently.   The truth is that if we were to go and pay our visit surreptitiously it might get Mut'ib into trouble, so I thought it best to put the matter to the test.   We now have a clear conscience, and I don't think anyone can interfere much with our amusement unless they take us openly as spies, and a little judicious teasing has made them feel that it is quite easy to look ridiculous!   It is so pleasant to feel that we have succeeded in doing what all the People who Know told us was impossible.   It appears that the Jebel is still under martial law and no one allowed in except with special permission. We told our friends at lunch that we meant to come again soon, and made them look rather glum.

Your own FREYA.

100.   *To her Mother.*

KANAWAT.   Monday, 14.5.28.

DEAREST B.,

You can't think what difficulties we have over these diaries, nor how exhausted we are from constant sociability. When our tour ends on Sunday, I think we shall be worn out, though happy.   We meant to have a long lazy rest in bed this morning; but they woke us, unnecessarily, at four; and at six we got up, knowing that if we waited to dress later we should have a divan of gentlemen looking on. We are now writing with a good-sized audience and hurrying to get as much down as possible.

It was pleasant to get away into freedom again.   I have kept my ideas on politics for the little book in Najm's tummy-band, but both V. and I feel we do not want to live in a French colony.   It is ridiculous to call this a mandate, for I believe there is not a Frenchman in the country who intends these people ever to govern themselves.   It is their bad manners that annoy me so.   They talk of them and to them as if they were scarce to be considered as human beings.   If the Druses ever get a chance, they will not leave a man of them alive in the whole district, and I have an idea that those who make the polite speeches will not be the last to join in the trouble.

Venetia was quite annoyed with the Mustashar for not coming to lift us into our donkey stirrups.   We offered him a ride on our nicest animal, the one that carries our bedding, but I don't think he likes to think of himself in conjunction with these undignified beasties.   It was delicious to be alone again : freedom and a breeze, and the plain below us; Leja, and Hermon, and the Hills of Brass, all our familiar landmarks.   Najm burst into a song with the joy of getting us again.   Even 'Arif's little face looked

M

broader than it is long. And the donkeys were well rested.

We had done with the flat land and the stones; it was the best sort of road, that wanders on the fringe of the hills, the lowlands on our right; and we soon left the big road and took a track for Suleime, and came upon it, with its solitary temple pillar in the foreground, and took our snapshots before entering the village.

Najm has relatives there: poor rough people. A nice man in a blue head-cloth with a long blond face, absurdly like Nicola at l'Arma, and devoted to his small only son. I have not yet seen a father caressing his daughter in this country.

I don't think Suleime can be a very healthy village: the children looked miserable and pale and dirty; we collected them as usual. The people seemed poor. We were apparently the first tourists known there in recent times. There is nothing to see except the one temple ruin which is going to topple over very soon. It must have been turned by the Moslems into a fort, for there are arrow-slits. In the fields around us we looked down into vaulted subterranean passages; the French had blocked the entrance to them during the Rebellion, and we were not enthusiastic enough for candles and investigation.

We tried to sleep after lunch. Najm had tied one donkey to the doorknocker, so that it was as if we were being lulled with castanets, and we got up fairly soon and went to visit the weaver who lives in a dark room rolling bright wool on to his clumsy loom. They have very attractive goat's-hair cushion stuff in dull orange patterns; we hope to find some in Suweida. We then called on the Sheikh. He did not seem very cordial, perhaps because we had not gone to him straight away: I think that is the sound policy in this country. It is very difficult: we have to pick up the etiquette as we go along.

The Sheikh's new house was plastered all over with fragments of the temple, bits of column or cornice or frieze let in anyhow into the walls. This vague appreciation of the antique is what is most rapidly ruining the old things here. As the temples fall they are dismembered and carried pell mell into other houses, and the villages are changing from year to year. I have seen some old columns at Kanawat to-day split half down their length and the hollow that served to hold the rod which joined one section to the other was made to serve as a water channel! An old man in the Sheikh's house at Suleime told us that a whole wall of the temple was standing when he was a boy, and he used to clamber about on it and look out for raiding Beduin. And he told us that there was a buried room under the very floor we were sitting on, with pillars and all intact, which was now completely blocked up and inaccessible.

When we left Suleime we at last came to trees. They were only the stumpy thorny-leaved things they here call oaks, but extremely joyful after five days without a sight of them. It was the first bit of shade we had seen outside a village since leaving Deir Ali and we insisted on celebrating it and sitting in it, and eating biscuits and enjoying Peace. You can't think what a strain it is to be practically never alone.

It was pleasant from Suleime up here: the hills in sight and we going up to them, and the temples of Kanawat shining out from green country; rolling slopes dotted with trees and vineyards. The track winds, very stony, between loose stone walls precariously balanced, and built one felt out of the ancient city, which must have stretched a long way. Porter[1] gives a careful description, but though we found all the single objects he describes, their position with regard to the town does not seem to tally. There is a beautiful temple, seven columns in a circle, as you come up; a castle on a hill to the left, and gentle slopes behind; the late light was on the grey stone of the pillars, standing above walnut trees; we looked over a wide prospect with Hermon faint beyond. Kanawat is really the best we have seen so far. The old temples live for their own loveliness among their orchards, grey stone carved with wreaths of vines or flowers, faded into soft colours, with nothing but the low black houses, themselves as old, to spoil the peaceful harmony.

[1] J. H. Porter, *Handbook for Travellers in Syria and Palestine*, 1875.

There is a little Roman theatre alone in a ravine, with the stream trickling by, and the remains of baths beside it; one can trace all the life of this little provincial town.   We have followed its main road up the valley, where the round towers of defence were built against the Arabs just as to-day, and the dead are gathered in heaped mounds of graves half lost under earth and grasses.   It is like surprising a secret soon to vanish for ever; the temples are crumbling, and if the country remains quiet enough to let the French look after it there will be horrors of red tiles and hideous hospitals before long.   The Mustashar told us that M. Ponsot liked red roofs and wants them all over the Jebel.   Beautiful Kanawat!   I am glad we have seen it.   But I must tell you in order.

We had a letter from the Mustashar to the High Priest of all the Druses, Sheikh Achmed el Hajari—apparently under the misguided impression that he is a friend of the French.   He is a keen old man with a fine aquiline profile and neat white beard still faintly blonde, and when Najm handed in our letter he seemed none too pleased with it till the news that we are not really French, but English, had a most happy effect.   I think he was troubled at the thought of having to entertain anything so unorthodox as two females alone, and sent us to his brother Sheikh Jussef next door, also a High Priest, and a jovial blackbearded man with a wife overlapping in rolls of fat who came to talk about her rheumatisms as it might have been on Dartmoor.

We then had an A.D.C. from Sheikh Achmed asking us in which house we should like to spend the night: these are such difficult problems to have to face unprepared. We decided on Sheikh Achmed and found ourselves in his guest-room with a table and two chairs prepared for us, and that is not nearly so comfortable as the round mat and little dishes on the floor.   And we had forks, so that Venetia's cleverness with her bread dipper was wasted.   I am clumsy, and cause much amusement.   Everything so far has been beautifully clean, far different from Damascus; and it is not really objectionable for all to drink out of the same two cups.

I think we disappointed the High Priest.   When he

heard that V. came from India, he and all the evening gathering became suddenly very eager and wanted her to explain the secret religions of the country. Unfortunately she is not at all up in these. I explained Buddhism as well as I could, and we then told them a little about Thibet and the Devil Worship of Central India: this was what they wanted and they were intensely interested and asked many questions, of which V. could not answer many. This was very disappointing, and I made matters worse by translating Devil Worship literally, and was surprised to hear a sort of groan of horror go round the room. I then remembered vaguely that the Druses do not believe themselves to be unique in the world, but hold that somewhere in the Far East there is another people of Druses who are coming as conquerors westward in the last days of the earth, to join their brothers in the Jebel. We were on delicate ground. I believe Sheikh Achmed had hoped that we came to him with a message. He gave us up as inadequate and gathered with the Elders round the table at the far end of the room where they read in low voices out of little green books, while the lesser men kept us amused. I have noticed by the way that these Elders will not shake a woman's hand if they can help it; we greet them by putting our hands to our breast, and that is evidently correct.

After supper the Sheikh left us, and the younger men asked if we would go with them to attend a wedding. We were just starting when the old A.D.C. came in and put his foot down very decidedly, considering it highly improper for ladies to walk about at night. We said that we were very tired (truthfully), and so we remained in the guest-room, and the Piper was sent for and we had war songs on the reed flute, wild songs that would make the Father of Quakers look about him for a bayonet. The men sat round with eyes shining.

When everyone had gone, the Sheikh and a fine-looking youngish man with a very keen face appeared again and asked if we would talk a little. I was so weary. But he began to question us about ancient graves, and especially he wanted to know what the town of Kanawat looked like in the ancient time. It was not antiquarian interest, but

some definite thing they were after and extremely eager
about: and we were disappointing again   I could tell
them nothing except that the buildings of this country are
not pre-Christian, which statement also I thought they
didn't like.   I have promised to try and procure photographs.   I would give something to know what it is they
are really thinking about.

One thing they told us pleased us hugely.   It seems that
only two English travellers have come into this district at
all since the Rebellion, and they were so shadowed they
were never able to see a Druse alone and returned having
seen practically nothing except French officers.   I believe
our freedom is due entirely to the Mustashar's fear of
making himself ridiculous.   I noticed it when I made a
foolish remark without any intention about it at all, but
he was so nervous, he immediately took it to himself: he
was shewing us snapshots and there was one of a long file
of camels led as usual by a donkey, and says I without
thinking: "*Ce n'est pas seulement les chameaux qui sont guidés
par les ânes*," and he looked so electrified I am sure he
thought I was referring to the Intelligence in the Jebel
Druse!   Anyway, here we are, beautifully free and
listening to Treason all day long.   One thing is undoubted:
Kanawat is not pro-French.

Your own FREYA.

101.   *To her Mother.*

SUWEIDA.   15.5.28.

DARLING B.,

We had such a flealess night in Kanawat, and were
allowed to go to bed so delightfully early, and the sense of
liberty with no police about was so charming, that we
decided to spend another day there.   We slept in the
guest-room.   The young men came back from the wedding,
one of them with an unorthodox blue ribbon round his
turban, for which he was reprimanded by the High Priest,
and made to dash it on the ground with a shamefaced air.
The Druse priests are elected and get no pay, but they enjoy
their authority.   After this little scene the men all trooped

out so that we might get into our beds, arranged in the window recess: the Sheikh himself superintended their making and then left us, and as the windows had shutters we were actually able to wash a little and take off some clothes, though that meant getting up very early next morning before the guest-room fills.

Next morning we wandered up the ravine described by Porter in 1875 and found it much the same—the little gem of a theatre with the stream running by, the baths, and the old tower above, now inhabited by the flute-player and his brother. We sat on carpets on a broad stone seat leaning against the old stone of the tower, and they gave us coffee and begged us to spend the next night there and brought me a little bottle of yellow Roman glass which had been dug out of the old floor inside, and which the Governor of Suweida had asked for in vain. I hope it may reach home safely. We looked across the ravine to the town straggling down the opposite slope and to what they call the Castle of Kanawat, a bit of old temple with high walls tottering.

Another young man, As'ad, came with us too and shewed us his little hoard of beads found in old tombs as he ploughed his fields; he wanted to pour them all in our laps, for he was an impetuous young Druse; but we only accepted one each and promised to remember him when we wear them: which we certainly will, for he was an engaging and handsome young villain, and lifted us over stone walls as if we were feathers in his hand; and had an attractive twinkle in his eye when he told us how they used to set the petrol of the French tanks on fire and wait to shoot the officers as they crawled out, or any little anecdote like that. He showed us as many wounds as were on the visible parts of him, and described the rest; and told us of two brothers and three cousins killed; and how they had aeroplane bombs over their heads all the time; and how the men left the village and lived among the rocks of the land around; "and what on earth could we do," said he, "when there were only 20,000 of us against all the French? Every ten years," said he, "we have a war." He said it with the air of being quite ready for the next when it comes. "The water is mad in our land"; that is how

he explained it.   I tried to keep clear of politics; but they
are all ready to confide them.   It is certainly a different atmosphere from that which surrounds the French
Intelligence.

As'ad took us over all the loveliness of Kanawat.   There
is a whole façade remaining of carved grey stone; delicate
work of traceries, but great cracks already shewing in it.
Another courtyard with Doric columns, and another
perfect doorway.   A little beyond, and just within the
old encircling wall, is an arched subterranean place
which may have been cisterns, and one column standing
near, the last of six which fell a few years ago and are those
I saw split up to carry water.   The old wall is still traceable
and stands clear on the east.   But everything is crumbling,
and I doubt if there will be anything left in twenty years
unless something is done by the government.   But even
the glories of Baalbek have no joy to give like this of
discovering your own ruins among the quiet fields and
streets, coming upon them unregarded though even here
dominant in their unrecognized loveliness.

Later As'ad took us walking near an hour to Sir at the
valley head.   He said it was ruined by Tamarlane: the
cannon of Tamarlane he said.   It is up on the hill and not a
stone standing.   We did not climb to it, but sat in a little
lonely temple down below, two windows and a vine-
wreathed door of carved stone.   It suddenly came upon me
that part of the beauty of Kanawat is that her stone is grey
and not black.   We wandered among the graves that lie
thick in the valley.   They all seem alike, mounds of stones,
rough built and round outside and contain a square
chamber with a carved entrance door, a pillar standing up
in the middle, and two recesses for bodies on each of the
three sides.   Many are broken in; many still untouched;
it must have been the graveyard of a wealthy town.   We
walked over the ploughed fields among the green corn and
the whole surface was broken with shards of red pottery
once buried with the dead.

We walked back by the old road between the loose walls
along the Roman water channel which they are now
digging out again for Kanawat to drink from.   The
ancient towers of defence, the bases only now remaining,

run all along the valley. The amount of building is amazing in all this poor land. Kanawat must have been a very big city with suburbs stretching far away. It is a peaceful place now, very green to our eyes after the stones of Leja. The vineyards spread on every side, the prostrate vines now green and shining in the sun, full of flower buds.

We lunched with As'ad, and then slept peacefully in his guest-room for two hours. Were then visited by the local secretary, an objectionable man with French education and slightly familiar manner who wanted to sit on our side of the hearth, but As'ad shooed him to his own place very promptly and decidedly. Chivalry is not a product exclusively European.

After this the Sheikh sent for us and we sat with him in his garden in lovely shade of walnut trees. How delicious it was! The great boughs threw a twilight over us and there was water trickling half unseen: poplars, pomegranates, figs, hawthorn and Batm (which I don't know); the Sheikh's fella-hin were running the water in small streams among his potatoes and beans. We talked about crops and answered questions about our riches: my income impressed him as great wealth, but Venetia, who was asked hers in terms of sheep and cows, he did not think much of; they do better in America, said he.

I have a horrid cough and cold which is nothing but fatigue; I find myself longing for silence, or to be able to tell Venetia to do the talking for a bit. I keep on forgetting that she knows no Arabic and must be translated to, and this must be trying for her; but the fact is that I am not fit for any extra labour. We are going along in pleasant harmony, which is remarkable considering the strain of extreme discomfort. I wonder if we shall remember how to behave if the Plumers or their A.D.C. invite us to lunch? When V. is meditative with downcast eyes, I now know that she is merely localizing a flea; and we have been a week without getting out of our clothes, and really don't mind.

I suddenly thought of asking to call on the Sheikh's wife last night, and we then realized that this had been expected of us all along. We were made very welcome and kept to supper with the lady. Her handmaid crouched a little

way off, and a feeble petroleum lamp gave light. There
is a disadvantage in eating with the women, and that is
that since they themselves have done the cooking they take
a particular pride in it and stuff your mouth with choicest
morsels. The Sheikh's wife was very genuinely kind.
There is a feeling of sisterhood which comes out in spite of
the difference of race and religion, and is pleasant to meet.
We had another good night after, and left this morning,
very sorry to see the last of Kanawat. We left our handsome box of Damascus sweets to the Sheikh's wife, and have
promised to send photos, enlarged the old man promptly
stipulated, of Sheikh Achmed himself and Ibrahim, his
son, and Hussein, the most tiresome baby grandchild I
have ever known.

We turned down again into the plain, hot already at
seven in the morning. A temple is recorded at 'Atyl: we
wanted to see it. But it is gone: built into a new square
house, the traceries and columns of the doorway let into the
wall and lost to all significance. One bit of column only
with a lovely capital remains at the head of some stairs.
There is a good tank in the village.

We went on, after a hasty cup of coffee with the Sheikh
and a few French words with the schoolmaster who came
rushing out with a khaki overcoat flung on like a toga and
looking very much like one of the more jovial Roman
emperors. He came from Lebanon, and had spent a
summer at Brumana, so we felt like friends at once.

It took us three hours, 5.45 to 8.45, from Kanawat to
Suweida: an old stony track, mostly between walls, below
the tree level and very hot.

Here we are in the Sheikh's house, and he is a charming
man, with a long nose and pointed black beard and flowing
white drapery round his turban—the picture of a gentle-
manly pirate.

Suweida itself is horrid. There is an abomination of a
red roof in it; streets of new houses (most of the old were
demolished during the fighting) and motors spinning on
the Damascus road. Things like bicycles in the shops;
and a restaurant; troops; and a feeling of bourgeois
militarism which seems characteristic of the French occu-

pation. We shall try to leave soon. We heard the war song of Shahba and saw a large group of cavalry, their red head-dresses showing well, moving up the valley. There is a public garden; spotless officers looking at us. Welcome is not exactly written on their faces. Our host, however, has some influence it seems with passports; he has taken ours and says we shall be allowed to go where we like with no trouble. If I knew the language and ways a little better, I rather think I could get through this country without a Frenchman ever knowing anything about it. Fun to try.

We are resting on nice soft mattresses. A mattress on the floor is really as comfy a bed as one can want. We start in a short while.

Your own FREYA.

102. *To her Mother.*

RESAS. 16.5.28.

DEAREST B.,

Suweida added the last outrage to our feelings by producing an Armenian Protestant who talked to us about Miss Strong. We felt that civilization was getting us, and were glad when our passports came and we could go. No one asked to see us: and we did not feel inclined to thrust ourselves on anybody's notice. I said we were going to see Mut'ib el Atrash in this little village, so that there should be no trouble after, especially for him; and as no one protested, here we are—about an hour and a half's ride along the edge of the plain. It is Hauran, a lovely rich cornland, soft green and brown, with a far gentle slope of hills to the south, and higher tells, wooded here and there, to the north and east; Tell el Kuleib, the hill of the small dog, rises highest, round and bare. Little tells spring up like tiny waves all over the plain, mostly with a village on them: they are still black stone, but not the fierce blackness of Leja.

A railway is just completed from the main Hejaz line to Suweida, but so far is only open to the military. As we came slowly down the hill by the main road, a kind Druse

joined with a helping hand on the donkey's rein and told
stories of the war.   Suweida was the centre of it all; the
garrison was besieged here for months, and two relieving
columns made away with before they could reach the hills.
This man spoke with great enthusiasm of a certain Colonel
Henry (I think it was colonel) who apparently keeps a
protecting hand over the Druses from across the border.
He said the English kept the Druse fugitives for a year, but
then got tired of them, and made them return; after
arranging, however, for their safety through this same
colonel, whom they now seem to consider as their accredited
guardian.

The man left us at the bottom of the hill.   Suweida and
Europe dropped away like a bad dream.   We rode at a
gentle pace, talking to two women also on donkeys.   A
man in a black 'abeya galloped past, his head swathed to
the eyes under his kafiye.   Najm hailed him and he turned:
he came from Azrak, where the refugees lived for a long
time, no doubt giving our Government a good deal to think
about.   I think this man had been in political difficulties.
He might have been a red-haired Crusader to look at.
Najm murmured about us, and he came up, very friendly.
Politics are not to be avoided.   He practically told me he
had come on a message "from over there": Ibn Sa'ud, I
took it.   "Did I know that Ibn Sa'ud had just been given
Ma'an by the English?"   I did not; and what had King
Abdullah to say to that?   "King Abdullah is rather
weak," my Crusader remarked.   He was very cheerful.
I wondered what was the particular mischief he was up to:
he evidently thought I was in it too.   The British officers
in Transjordan are charming, he told me; but my Arabic
is better than theirs—which I hope is not true, for the
credit of our service.   We passed a clear spring welling up
under a rock: a good sight that is.   He watered his horse;
after a couple of hundred yards we came to one of the long
black tents in the open field.   We noticed a great to do:
welcomes, questions, someone bidding us to dismount: this
was Mut'ib's house and we had arrived at Resas.

I can't tell you how charming these people are to us.
Mut'ib's old servant was Salehmy's nurse, and she comes

from Brumana and fell upon our necks. They are all
camped here: the big house in their village close by is still
in ruins: the French blew up all the Atrash houses with
dynamite. They were their chief enemies, and Mut'ib is
only four months home from exile. Sultan el Atrash, the
head of the clan, being no longer wanted by the British in
Transjordan, has now gone south to Ibn Sa'ud: I have a
shrewd suspicion that our red-haired friend was bringing
news of him. Mut'ib is a kindly-looking man with a
drooping black moustache and a gentle smile and a
masterful wife. His cloak is full of bullet-holes. He says
that its dust-colour makes him difficult to hit and the
looseness catches the bullets in its folds. He explains this
with the rather shy enthusiasm of a man talking about his
hobbies. His son is like him, and just as amiable, only
very deaf. Salehmy's letter has given us the welcome of
dear friends: they are dreadfully put about that we can
only be received in the open tent, and have devoted all
the mattresses they usually sleep on themselves to making
us a soft bed while they take the hard ground. They will
not hear of our leaving to-day, and we are very happy
here. We have taken our writing to the top of a little hill
where a wind is moving the dry grasses, and we are having
a spell of quiet.

Of course there is no pretence of neutrality here. One
can't expect people to sit beside their ruined homes and
talk nicely of the people who did the mischief, and cut
down all their trees into the bargain. The village is
mostly knocked to bits, and they point to every other
village round about with some bloodthirsty anecdote:
pacifists the Druses are not. The sight of a gun is like the
huntsman's horn to a hunter! The fighting in Suweida,
so they say, was three thousand Druse against eight
thousand French, and an English colonel taking cinema
pictures while the battle raged. If this were true, no
wonder relations might be strained! The Druses lived
long among the rocks, till these—our friends—got across
the border to Azrak and stayed a year, as told above. It
was then that Sultan went to Ibn Sa'ud while Mut'ib and
his wife chose exile in Brumana, whence they have now
come home to their children and fields. They are busy

sowing maize, all the family in the tent with their servants and animals round them. There is Mut'ib, his wife and son, and his sister the Emir Hassan's wife, divorced—an immense lady with slanting eyes and brows, still with an imperious and untrustworthy beauty which must have been most alarming and wonderful before she grew so stout. There are also four small grandchildren with blackened eyes and grimy little faces, followed round by a brown-skinned Beduin woman who has come to Mut'ib for protection against her husband who wants to kill her.

An absurd coincidence is going to plunge us more than ever into the bad books of the authorities. A lady journalist from the *Figaro* is making the tour of Syria and has reached Suweida. All the notables were invited to speak to her this morning, and Mut'ib has started with the intention of telling exactly what he thinks of things. Our arrival yesterday is timed exactly to make us appear abettors in this expression of feeling.

We talked of many things last night in the guest-room of the tent with one side open to the evening as darkness crept down the hills. The women sat with us, rather careless about their veils, for there was only Najm, and he is a distant relation, and besides, these are great ladies and less troubled than lesser folk by conventions. We drank coffee over the primus stove and Mut'ib told me about the Druse religion—a little. There are five million Druses in India, he says, living under another name. My guess in Kanawat was correct. There are Druses in Algiers, Constantinople, and Philadelphia, where, he says, they go by the name of Quakers. The idea of Mr. Fox as a Druse filled me with joy. I asked Mut'ib whether he meant the Druses who, like all Syrians, emigrate in great quantities to the States; but he said no, they are an independent sect of Druses called Quakers. He was a little shaken when I told him that the masters at Brumana school are mostly Quakers; and more dubious still when I said that Quakers are non-combatants. "Then they cannot be real Druses," said he.

We were being eaten alive meanwhile, and were very languid for food: ten hours since the last meal, and it was

9.30 and the talk going round to the Divinity of Christ; I felt the words wandering from me in a mist; it had gone on solidly for three hours. Lucky Venetia who could be silent, drooping in the shadow of her hat; and 'Arif, who just curled himself on the floor and slept! Venetia says that the first three mouthfuls of dinner gave my voice quite a different ring! It was a splendid dinner: chicken on rice, beans, rice pudding, coffee, the delicious coffee freshly made which we shall miss so often.

The bed was made up in our dining-room; three mat-tresses and two yellow quilts. We were taken out by the nurse from Lebanon for a little preliminary walk into the landscape . . . with a lantern; picking our way among sleeping animals in the starlight. The whole tent looked very busy and homelike, lighted up, as the servants moved here and there preparing for the night, the five divisions shewing open like the rooms in a doll's house. Delicious sleep in a tent; with the camel tethered outside, and the gentle flap of the hair cloth in the night wind; the sense of great spaces around us, and silence and the nearness of the stars. Mut'ib has ideas, too, of Western requirements and tied a sheet across the open side, so that we slept undisturbed till 5.30, when the sun came up over the shoulder of Kuleib.

Your own FREYA.

103. *To her Mother.*

SALHAD. 17.5.28.

DEAREST B.,

Our day finished very quietly yesterday—one of the best we have had. One would get very fond of that broad land, treeless but full of lights and swelling lines like the sea. We took a family group of Mut'ib and his grand-children and then wandered a little in the sunset. We have not been so comfortable anywhere in our travels, not even in the official luxury of Shahba. And we grew fond of our hosts. To-day, as we trudged along a stony land in the heat, Najm told me the story of Iachya Bey, the father of our hostess, who rode with a friend from Damascus to Suweida bearing a letter to the Wali there from the Turkish governor. The letter gave orders for the bearer to be poisoned. As they went along the two friends both had suspicions, and Iachya's companion suggested breaking the seal before going any further; but Iachya refused. The Suweida Wali was his friend, and unwilling: he put the poison in the cups, but made a signal by wringing his hands. Iachya's comrade understood and poured the coffee under his kafiye, and was saved; but Iachya drank: he left the house, and fell dead a few steps down the street.

Najm told me this in the hottest and stoniest of wildernesses this morning because I was objecting to his reading my letters to the notables here. And because we have been cross with him he is suffering from headache and depression. We began to be annoyed yesterday when he set about shaving just in front of us. I don't see why anyone should do that without asking permission just because he happens to be a Druse! Then he woke us at four this morning and kept us waiting, crosser and crosser, till six for our breakfast! I ask you. Then he forgot to fill our bottles with the good water, and his table manners are sometimes insupportable; and finally we do not see why he should always ride and little 'Arif walk. Now he has another and better reason for depression, for our French letter has brought us to the house of a genuinely francophil Druse, the father of the Interpreter at Shahba, and an enemy of Mut'ib's. I would not have come if I had known. He began to speak of Mut'ib, and I had to shut him up and say that he was our friend and that we had eaten in his house.

Your own FREYA.

104. *To her Mother.*

SALHAD. 18.5.28.

DEAREST B.,

We had a long ride yesterday—six hours, ending at 1 p.m., all stones and not a tree. We climbed up into the hills again and found Hebron, a beautifully high-placed village with old doors and carvings scattered about but no building intact in particular: it must have changed a great deal since Porter's day. Below it was a big shallow lake full of sweet-smelling water flowers; women washing clothes and boys playing, riding bareback donkeys; as gentle a scene as is possible in the land of black stone. Venetia walked round to get a picture, while I sat on Iateem—it is I who call my small donkey the Orphan—sucking an orange, and was just handing the skin down to his little grey muzzle, for he has a passion for it, when an old man came and begged it for his children. Oranges are the extreme of luxury in the Jebel. I got him a fresh one out of the bag and left him very pleased.

We rode along a rough track over stony country. A man on a camel followed us, swaying on his high saddle in the sun; it looks as if the movement should hypnotize one completely. We came to a little stream, and shepherds with flocks, and there cut into the road from Suweida to Salhad. Shossa they call it here, and I puzzled over the etymology till I suddenly thought it must be from "*chaussée.*" Its surface is not even, but Syrian cars do not mind it. We met one, but it seemed to take nothing from the loneliness.

It got hotter and hotter, Salhad was invisible and ever farther off. A desolate land of grey stones in heaps. At our back was the central group of the Jebel, Kuleib rising from among it with smooth reddish slopes. The colours in these volcano rocks, and the sun and the distances threw an enchantment over the barrenness. We passed one village on our left, and people, and camels grazing with frisking foals on a strip of greenness. We thought we should never reach Salhad. But we turned a corner at last and saw it unexpectedly, a great Arab pile on a hill jutting into the plain; another hill opposite on the south, also jutting out, gives it the aspect of a gateway through which the Roman road runs straight from Bosra to Salhad, from Salhad to the desert.

Our host is a talkative, plausible man, with an eye for the things of this world, full of hospitality and enthusiastic for the French. His eyes are heavily blackened and his teeth profusely gilded, and he lives in an old vaulted

Roman bath which, he says truly, is not attractive as a dwelling but he is fond of it because it came to him from his father. His country house is what he is proud of, and he has been planting trees there; and he is proud of his one son and was pleased to hear news of him; and told us that he was going to send him to finish his education as a *concierge* in America, and that he was all in favour of civilization. He shewed us all the process of the coffee-making, cooked and poured in diminishing quantities through four coffee-pots, the last flavoured with cardamom and verbena. His are the genuine old coffee-pots; made with no join out of one sheet of brass; he showed us how to know them; and they had beautiful handles of brass and leather plaited together very small. A nicely kept coffee hearth is a pleasant sight. In the great houses the fire is always ready burning, but mostly there are only the ashes, and a little burning charcoal is brought quickly when the guest arrives.

We had a letter to the Salhad Intelligence lieutenant, and went up the village after our meal to hand it in. We passed a tank as big as a small lake and climbed up the straggling street through crowds of Moroccan troops until we met the surprising vision of a fair young man in tennis clothes walking along with a racquet. This was Philip Effendi, the Interpreter, a charming Greek from Cyprus, and a British subject; he sees nothing at all strange in our predilection for donkeys, and does not think us spies, and is the first man we have met to talk at all rationally about things here. I believe he feels exactly as we do about the military. We had to wait a long time before we could get a permit from the Commandant of the garrison to visit the citadel, and he murmured to me that: "Soldiers have too much imagination; they always see things that are not there." He took us to see the Intelligence man, Lieutenant Henri, who is a Norman and even more handsome to look at than the Interpreter. He cannot be more than twenty-two or twenty-three. All the Intelligence Officers out here seem to be very young.

We were invited to dinner, and then finally got the permit for the citadel, and a soldier took us climbing up a long steep way through barbed wire, the whole place like a rabbit warren for troops and guns: the ugly black muzzles stick out at every angle, with ammunition stacked close by and the sentinels in readiness. It was very like war days. A concentration camp on our left as we climbed, with eighty Druses behind the wire living in tents. They say it is only during the last four months that the country has become safe at all; and Salhad is near the eastern edge of it. Not a tourist place, we felt: though two Americans have been here before us.

The old fortress is round, the slanting outer ramparts fairly intact, but everything crumbled away inside: the garrison has scooped out rooms and dug-outs among the debris, and gun emplacements to sweep the land. The view is unforgettable: the hills of the Jebel like waves on the north and west, and Hermon far away with the sunset behind him. We looked down on to the black flat roofs of the town, a sheer drop; then out into the sunset-coloured plain, where the straight road ran like an arrow, out to the very borders of Law. Our castle shadow lay on it like an immense triangle. We stayed watching while the evening turned to blue dusk. There is something threatening in that emptiness.

We had a very agreeable evening. We were given water to wash in, and eau de Cologne and a mirror, every luxury. My throat makes it agony to talk, or I should have enjoyed it more. Our Druse was there too, so that his feelings might not suffer at our absence from his house: a very different attitude from that of Shahba. Lieutenant Henri and his Interpreter are in fact gentlemen, and I think they were as pleased as we to sit and talk of books and Paris and the pleasant things of life. They were interrupted at their meal and had to leave us. Beduin raiders had come across the border to loot camels at about four hours' distance on horseback. We heard details this morning: there were twelve raiders and they carried off the camels from some Druse Beduin. The native police followed and killed them all, losing three of their own men and six wounded, and apparently two French non-commissioned officers wounded, but we were not able to know this for certain. Lieutenant Henri told me that these things happen in summer, as soon as food is becoming scarce. He was very polite, but it is evident that they all consider British laxity in Transjordania to be responsible for these irregularities. We did not feel it a good moment to uphold the Expression of Individuality! This morning they have all been taken up with the burial of the poor men; riding of posts and champing of bits and galloping horses. The Intelligence Officer has come over from Suweida and looked at us suspiciously, asking how we got through without his knowledge: this is more than we can tell him. We should have liked to attend the burial, but were not invited: which makes one rather think there may be some truth in the story of French casualties. Our host here says that the Druses never pray over the dead who have died in battle.

We had no time to wander over Salhad town last night. This morning the lieutenant tempted us with the offer of a real tub, and the road to Bosra looks so dusty and monotonous, that we decided to let Najm go on with the donkeys while we take things easily and follow by car.

We are running out of films, and took only two photos: the lions carved on the old gate-posts and the mosque and its minaret, which is a charming little hexagonal tower. The mosque has only its arches left. The little town is different from the others we have seen, for it seems to be completely Moslem; inscriptions everywhere, and stone window lattices, primitive' but good: we have not seen these elsewhere.

Your own FREYA.

105.　*To her Mother.*

BOSRA ESKI SHAM. 18.5.28.

DEAREST B.,

We have come to Bosra by car, a very flat, dull road, and we are now in the Sheikh's house. We have left the Druses; they are all Moslems here. The house very grand with glass window-panes and chairs (though we don't use them). Dozens of children and flies, and one of the children's hair being combed, filling us with anxiety

and discomfort. The town has an immense castle, also
Saracen—thirteenth century—and it looks as if there were
many lovely things, but we must wait till it gets cooler.
It was 37 Cent. in the shade, and is hotter now; and I
cannot shake off my disgusting throat. How nice it will
be to lie in bed in Jerusalem and look at clean clothes
ready for one!

Your own FREYA.

106. *To her Mother.*

TRANSJORDANIA. 19.5.28.

DARLING B.,

Our only experience of a night among the Moslems
was rather awful. We never thought there were so many
varieties of biting things, and longed for the morning; and
we slept in the harem with two ladies whose mattress was
close to ours, so that we could not fling Keating's about
too openly.

Bosra is a wonderful old town; a Roman provincial
capital with the straight road running to its ancient gate
and ruins on either hand. There are great parts of it
uninhabited on either side of the old pavement. The city
gate is ruined, but on the way down to it one goes by a
perfect arch still standing, lovely in proportion. That also
is cracked right across. A little off the main road is the
Christian church, which became a mosque: we sat among
the columns, their marble yellow and rose-coloured in the
evening light, and the make of the old stone roof shewing
very clearly. The little tower was also roofed with stone.
None of this building is younger than the fifth century.

We found another little gem of a mosque, also a con-
verted church it must have been. The stone slabs of its
doors are intact and the stone trellis windows. An old
tree and temple columns stand beside it, and a square
stone tower; and here Muhammed, in his youthful travelling, is said to have first learnt about Christianity from
an old monk in Bosra—a doubtful story.

But the castle is the best of all. It is a mass of huge
square buildings with a fosse round, and a bridge, and the

Saracens built it round the Roman theatre. We have become familiar with garrisons now. We never hesitated to go up and say that we wished to look over their citadel, which is armed to the teeth, like Salhad. The two officers we applied to themselves conducted us, after calling an Algerian trooper with a lamp. The whole centre of the theatre is filled in and three great halls built in it; one above the other, the lowest not yet explored and none of them lighted (except perhaps the top one). We climbed down by the theatre steps and along the subterranean passages which once ran round the tiers of seats. Here and there some marble columns gleam under the lamp, walled in the rough stone. The old porticoes were turned by the Arabs to defence. In the heart of the place is a dark damp mosque built by Saladin, with an inscription; and there are Arabic lines running round the outer walls too. The Algerians look well with their baggy light uniforms and turbaned heads under the old walls and arches. We saw them riding through the streets of the town, a splash of colour, on high medieval saddles, with the black-bearded Moslems scowling at them from their doors.

As we came away I stopped to look at a stone built into the wall of a house. It gave the name of the third legion. The French Intelligence officer beside me told me that this was the Gallic Legion. He said it as if the French had been settled here ever since. A terribly dangerous thing is history.

They have a curious ornament over many of the Bosra gateways: a kind of small parapet built out of mud and straw, and little flags stuck into it, ostrich feathers and long streamers of any old stuff. All I could discover about them is that they are put up when a boy is born in the house.

We got home quite late and sat down to wait for supper. It is the stranger host's duty to put himself about for his guests, and our twelve days have taught us to take this for granted. But after the respect and friendliness of the Druses, we felt our female inferiority rather acutely among the Moslems, for we sat with the women on the far side of the coffee hearth and the men came dropping in, heavily bearded and fierce to look at, and never spoke to us; and when the coffee was ready they all drank first, and then sent only the little son of the house in his long blue gown and bare feet to carry us the cups. The women, dressed in blue like the Beduins or the Christians of Leja, sat with us unveiled.

There was a sensation, however, before we reached the coffee stage. The door was flung open and two native soldiers strode in. All sprang to their feet except Venetia and I. They came up and asked us to spend the evening with the Commandant in the fortress. The Arabs, all standing in a circle, waited for our reply. It was already late, and it meant going right across the dark town with two rough-looking soldiers, and insulting our host by leaving his coffee untasted; and all to see uninteresting Frenchmen. We excused ourselves politely. The soldiers looked with stupefaction. You might have heard a pin drop in the room. After a prodigious pause, one of them exclaimed: "You are women; and tired: the Commandant will pardon you"; then they turned on their heels and left.

Silence followed. The assembly settled back to continue the interrupted evening; but we felt it was a moral victory, and that our audience was pleased. Presently the lady of the house murmured that we were quite right not to "venture at night among the French soldiers," which view of the question had not struck us. As no British ladies are remembered to have stayed here before, I hope we may have established a national reputation for propriety!

We were taken to sleep in the harem. The Sheikh's young wife was having her hands tattooed; they were caked over with wet earth and tied up in rags, and she and her friend lay on a mattress close beside us. The mother-in-law locked us in with a big key which she afterwards threw in through the window. Half-way through the night we could bear it no longer, and thought we would risk the wickedness of the Moslems rather than suffocation. We consulted with the ladies, and unlocked the door (with some trepidation because of mother-in-law): we flung it wide and were able to breathe.

This morning our host gave us the most friendly send-off. Our humiliation was due to our sex and not personal. He told us that the greatest pleasure we could ever give him was to come and stay again, and pressed my hand over and over: and I feel sure it is because of what we said to the soldiers. We sat for a while watching the mounted troops out in the open manœuvring: wild galloping squares and circles, the dust flying, the sun catching the red and white as they turned.

There is a railway line at Bosra, and we said good-bye to Najm at the station; to Najm and 'Arif and our three little donkeys. A sad parting. Najm will travel slowly home by Damascus.

Your own FREYA.

107. *To her Mother.*

APPROACHING JERUSALEM. 20.5.28.

DARLING B.,

We are now climbing up from Jericho to Jerusalem— a boiling drive through desolate hills that look as if all life had deserted them centuries ago.

We did not take the smart little train from Bosra after all, but a car which bumped us along an hour or so earlier. It was no pleasure falling among Christian chauffeurs again—what a set of bragging, inefficient persons we have had since yesterday! We got rid of the first little man at Der'aa with thankfulness, and after having our passports seen to there—no difficulties at all over our leaving the country, and much politeness—we asked the obliging Armenian waiter if he could not get a car for Jerusalem. A six-hours' ride in a 1928 Hudson was promised us. The outside of this model was not so varnished and shining as one might expect, but the chauffeur and his club-footed young brother seemed full of confidence and cheerfulness.

At the first village, Remte, King Abdulla's policeman discovered one passport missing; he was obliging and let the boy through after taking his name. They are fine-looking police with their chain-mail shoulder straps, and have been all the military in sight so far: a contrast to Syria. At Irbid, the next little town, we stopped again and were asked to change into a miserable, uncomfortable little

Dodge car: we refused: the village gathered round and
tried explanations in every language; we continued to
refuse in bad but positive Arabic and explained that the
car was ours till Jerusalem, and we meant to sit in it till we
got there. Seeing us obstinate, the village finally decided
we must be right. The little Dodge went off packed with
more Arabs than it was intended to hold, and we went
happily along in great spirits and harmony till our first
puncture; it was soon mended, but we here discovered
that we had no spare wheel except an ancient object
apparently put on for ornament.

We went through very lovely rich country, deep valley
cuts and up again among hills; gradually to trees and real
woods, through corn waving in loneliness, so that one
wonders who comes to reap there. The villages are the
warm yellow of the Damascus mud-building: we stopped
at one to get water: a fair young Beduin girl drew it up
for us from the covered well, looking very ancient and
clothing even the old petroleum tin she used as a bucket
with the poetry of the old stories: she would take no money
for the hard labour.

Suddenly, just as I had been drowsing in the hot afternoon, we turned a corner and saw the temples and pillars
of Jerash lying in a cup of the yellow hills above the trees
and stream which divide them from the new town: you
can't imagine more lovely ruins: a long Roman street
ending in a circular forum of Corinthian pillars, nearly all
standing; as you walk along the ancient pavement you
see the whole length of the street, the ruts of ancient carts,
the great fountain, a gateway, and the other steep street
leading from the bridge to the temple of Astarte, whose
orange-coloured pillars stand high above against the sky.
Theatres and baths and gates—they are all there, half
overgrown with plants and coloured to indescribable
loveliness: still unspoilt, though an Italian engineer and
an American mission are working there and will soon take
away the perfect charm; they are restoring the great gate,
but so far it is still the ancient town half lost in its lonely
hillside, its pillars and stones the same warm yellow of the
landscape, its secrets still left to the imagination.

We walked up and down the ancient street, and called on the engineer, Signor Ricci, a nice little mild man with an artistic pointed beard and untidy hair, and a discrimination in beautiful things rather refreshing after life among the Druses.   He gave us orange water in a room full of lovely carpets and weavings and talked about the worked stones one sees so often here, the edges chiselled and centre left rough: apparently this was a Greek invention, as they used to smooth over their stones *after* placing them, and so discovered the effectiveness of leaving the rough centres.   I saw these stones at Jubeil and Salhad, and in lots of places.   The system of shoving old bits of columns into their walls, lengthways like sausages, was, it seems, typically Mahommedan; one sees that often, also, and it has an absurdly undignified effect.

Your own FREYA.

108.   *To her Mother.*

JERUSALEM.   20.5.28.

DARLING B.,

We found our chauffeur very cross when we had loitered over an hour in Jerash, and discovered that he had been inventing the "six hours" to Jerusalem and that we could not think of getting there under seven or eight.   He had also drunk the water from our water bottle and filled it with a horrid-looking turbid liquid.   He began to feel that we did not like him.   When the second puncture found us on a great lonely height near sunset, and Venetia discovered that he had not the faintest notion of the inside of a car, we liked him even less, and his brother less than him.

We had a wonderful drive: it is all a huge country, and the road keeps high up, looking down into steep wadis, now red with oleanders: we left the olives and pines and oak trees and came again to bare country, but grand, and in colour lovely browns like some gigantic Dartmoor in its russety seasons.   A glorious country to ride over: lonely but not wild—perhaps the feeling of the good road, and the views of it from inside a car, took its wildness away: and when we did come to a village, it had glass windows and electric light, and it was at the peaceful moment when the cattle come home to their stables. We stopped at a spring outside to fill up with water. We realized by now that the radiator leaked, and I spoke with an old Arab and discovered that my language goes well enough this side of the border also.

By the time we reached Es Salt it was dark: we could only see a fine pile of houses built up the hillside. We had had no lunch—only an orange and biscuits—and even our tummies, now so well trained, were feeling languid. When it came to lighting the lamps, of course these were all out of order: we spent a long time over that and then sped down carefully (for it was evidently the man's first drive by night) into the Jordan valley, the air coming in hot blasts off the rock, as hot as the air from an oven. It was like descending into hell, the black valley and fierce hot air. The last village before Jericho was already on the flat strip of Jordan land: there were people sitting round lamps at supper, as little clothed as they could be in the stifling heat. Our chauffeur, now rather dazed with fatigue and stupidity, found us four raw eggs, which we sucked: they were tepid and not really attractive. Then we made for Jordan across sandy flat land broken into clefts, overgrown with tamarisk bushes (I think) that sprang suddenly into the lamplight. The fierce air grew hotter and hotter.

The road was marked by stones, but the man was always losing it and the tamarisk bushes seemed to close in round him. I stopped him just in time—we were going over into one of the steep little ravines, were close upon the edge of it in fact. I think he was thoroughly demoralised, and it was a most fantastic ride. We got to the long wooden covered bridge over Jordan about nine o'clock; were let through by the Transjordan police with lots of advice, but all heterogeneous; saw a gleam of water in the starlight; found the chain already up on the Palestine side and an amiable but I believe slightly drunk policeman who suggested accompanying us. "Is it only clothes in your luggage? Never mind," says he, and with this strange remark we shoot off among the tamarisks again, but on the good road this time, and reach Jericho near ten o'clock. We found a very clean, pleasant little hotel, trying to feel cool by calling itself Winter Palace: we had tea and marmalade for breakfast, after tea and ginger beer at supper: we felt we were in British territory.

This morning we caught just one glimpse of the Dead Sea, a solid grey-blue among the dead streaks of its mountains. You climb up through these hard ranges, no vegetation, nothing but the hot baked rock, till you reach the high land—a few olives, a few stubbly patches of wheat, new square religious buildings on the hillsides, and then Jerusalem suddenly, all its varieties of architecture and beliefs gathered in the squareness of the medieval walls: it was impressive in an unexpected way and in spite of all the ugly details.

We have settled in at the Franciscan hospice—Casanova —and sent all our accumulated clothes to be washed, and feel incredibly luxurious. Venetia went to get our nice clothes from the agent, and came back with the surprising news that it is Sunday. It is two weeks since we reached Damascus: and we have never counted time as a positive matter in this interval. How good it has all been: the discomforts vanish, at least from *active* memory; and the loveliness of it all remains and grows. And the joy is that I have been able to do it after all, and the silly old body has really played up rather well considering.

We shall take it easy now—rest complete for two days, then send my letter to the Governor's A.D.C. and try to put ourselves into decent clothes again. It is nice of me to go about with Venetia because, of course, no one looks at me when she is about: perhaps there will be enough charming young men to go round.

Love to you both, dear B. I hope my writing is not too illegible.

Your own FREYA.

109. *To Miss Buddicom.*

ASOLO. 23.6.28.

DEAREST VENETIA,

I have just had a note from Mr. E. in Brumana. He says we have left "a trail of surmises and not a little dust"; that the people there "fail to see why you should choose to live and perhaps die in the slums of Damascus merely because you wish to learn Arabic. Neither can they see why you should choose to stay in a native household, rather than at a public hotel of known repute in the company of a wide circle of English, French, and German-speaking people. As for the venture in the Desert, that indeed is difficult to understand! Is it likely that you would wish to risk your skin merely to see a pile of ugly old ruins, and is it likely that your friend would wish to risk her skin merely to keep you company? And why should you be so friendly with the Druses? And anyway why are you so specially interested in people who must still be regarded as something of a menace to the existing government? And how did you manage to get such valuable introductions?" He ends: "I merely repeat the sort of rumours that have been floating about. If you should ever come out here again before you are completely forgotten, you will be a character crusted over with quite a mythology: people will knit their troubled brows in obvious perplexity."

So that's that!!

Have you heard about Liverpool sailings? It will be for end of September I should say.

Your loving FREYA.

110. *To Miss Buddicom.*

BRUMANA. 8.10.29.

DEAREST VENETIA,

It was very like old times going to see Najm yesterday. I found his house in the middle of a crimson sunset on the other side of Brumana ridge, and three little girls playing about the doorstep. Najm's wife was there and I was just explaining myself when a large lady overwhelmed me with embraces, and turned out to be the Nurse of Resas, the one in whose house Najm shaved so much to your annoyance. Najm himself was having a bath and soon appeared swathed in white and very cordial, and I had a great time hearing the news and all the complications that followed us. Najm had been back for some months trying to set up a shop in Suweida and saw all our friends— and *none* of them ever received a single photo!! Isn't this too bad. I said I would write at once and ask you to send a new lot, and I am meanwhile writing to Kanawat and Resas to explain.

Najm declares that he wrote to me twice, and of course I never received the letters. Well, he told me he went to Shahba with a load of samn, and happened to meet the Mustashar, who stopped him and said: "Who are you? I seem to know your face." Najm explained, and the Mustashar told him that it was lucky for Najm that we left when we did, as he was going to put him in prison for a month, the reason being partly because he had told us of the cross-questionings that had been inflicted on him and so let us know that we were under suspicion; and partly because someone had reported what the man at Salhad had said against Mut'ib and how we had snubbed him, and a furious quarrel had sprung up in consequence.

The Mustashar has since been in Beirut and came up here and visited Najm in a friendly way, so all is well; and is now somewhere up the coast, just where I should like to travel in the Spring. I think I may call on him some time and see what he is like under less trying circumstances.

I am going for a four days' trek across the hills to the source of the Stream of Adonis, and shall then follow it down to the sea. Will let you hear.

Dear love to you,

FREYA.

111. *To Miss Buddicom.*

BRUMANA. 15.10.29.

DEAREST VENETIA,

I have had four glorious days on a mule with Najm up over the hills to Afka and down the Adonis stream. I found two great temples. No columns standing, but only the tracing of the walls. I did miss you so! I also came to the conclusion that I *cannot bear* Najm's table manners when I have them all to myself!

He told me by the way that we really had been very lucky in the matter of escaping raids on our trip. At Redeme the road was only just clear of bandits. They had come by night, and though the people had weapons they could not use them for fear of letting the authorities know that they possessed them; but they caught and beat the thieves and handed them over to the police. Whereupon the bandits who escaped infested that bit of road we trotted along in the dark! and they had only just been cleared away. Then, on the way back, Najm had to make a long detour, as the east of Leja was unsafe altogether. So we were really very carefully guarded by that immoral Providence which attends the reckless.

I hope I shall reach Baghdad with all my luggage intact. I am economizing and going by a native car instead of the official Nairn.

Your loving FREYA.

INDEX

1. Lindos, Rhodes (*page 11*)

2.   Coastal hills of Syria (*page 49*)

3. Asphodels over Syrian ruins

4. Flocks of the Beduin (*page 118*)
   Hawking in Syrian cornfields

5. Cutting the corn

6. Roman ruins at Baalbek (*page 129*)

7. Great Mosque, Damascus (*page 103*)

8. In a Damascus bazaar (*page 107*)

9. A cobbler at Damascus (*page 117*)

10. Escort first seen (*page 129*)

11. Freya Stark, Najm and 'Arif (*page 132*)

12.   Groups at Deir Ali (*page 132*)

13.   Stone doors at Burak (*page 139*)

14. Freya Stark and 'Arif by the well at Redeme (*page 144*)
Inside the guest room at Redeme (*page 145*)

15. Beduin girl dancing near Shahba (*page 154*)
     Coffee pots (*page 121*)

16.   School children at Redeme (*page 147*)

17. Miss Buddicom and French officers at Shahba (*pages 150-152*)

18.   Circular temple at Kanawat (*page 163*)

Little theatre in the ravine (*page 164*)

19. Ruins at Kanawat (*page 168*)

20. Ruins at Kanawat (*page 168*)
     Temple ruins below Sir (*page 168*)

21. The castle guard at Bosra (*page 181*)
Children in gateway at 'Atyl (*page 170*)

22. Mut'ib and his grandchildren at Resas (*page 175*)
Making butter at Resas

23. Mut'ib's tent at Resas (*page 172*)
Ruined mosque and minaret at Salhad (*page 180*)

24. Bosra (*page 181*)